Black Foremothers

Three Lives

Black Foremothers

Three Lives

Second Edition

Dorothy Sterling

Foreword by Margaret Walker
Introduction by Barbara Christian

The Feminist Press
at The City University of New York
New York

94 93 92 91 4 3 2

Library of Congress Cataloging-in-Publication Data

Sterling, Dorothy, 1913–
  Black foremothers.

  Bibliography: p.
  Includes index.
  1. Afro-American women—Biography. 2. Craft, Ellen,
3. Wells-Barnett, Ida. B., 1862–1931. 4. Terrell,
Mary Church, 1863–1954. I. Title.
E185.96.S75 1987   973'.0496073022 [B]   87-19746
ISBN 0-935312-89-7

Cover design by Lucinda Geist

Cover art: *Left:* courtesy of the University of Chicago Library, Department
of Special Collections, Ida B. Wells Papers (89). *Top row, left to right:*
courtesy of Julia DeCosta (35); courtesy of the University of Chicago
Library, Department of Special Collections, Ida B. Wells Papers (88);
courtesy of *Afro-American Newspapers* (138); Library of Congress (139).
Bottom row, left to right: The Underground Railroad by William Still, 1872,
American History Division, New York Public Library, Astor, Lenox, and
Tilden Foundations (34); courtesy of New York Public Library Picture
Collection (35); courtesy of *Afro-American Newspapers* (138); courtesy of
the University of Chicago Library, Department of Special Collections, Ida B.
Wells Papers (88). The numbers in parentheses indicate pages on which
further information can be found.

Distributed by The Talman Company, 150 Fifth Avenue, New York, NY 10011.

Table of Contents

DA

Foreword

HERE IS A BOOK OF BIOGRAPHIES that is unique in many ways. Its advent can be compared to that of Gertrude Stein's fictional book of the same name, *Three Lives*, which contains the first serious study of a black woman (Melanctha) in white American literature. This book presents not one but three black women, all of them real people. Biographies of three black women? Why? How did this unusual event happen? There are four immediate answers: Dorothy Sterling; The Feminist Press; the civil rights movement; and the women's movement.

Dorothy Sterling is highly qualified to do these biographical studies. For the past quarter of a century, she has researched the history of American black people and has written narratives of that history. Her work was a part of the earliest stirrings of the civil rights movement. By the 1960s, that movement had forced a general reconsideration of black history that is still in progress and that resulted in an increasing visibility of black men in our nation's history books. If the black woman is now to become visible and valued in our history, it will be as the result of the women's movement that arose in the 1970s. But without publication efforts such as The Feminist Press has undertaken here, recognition of the black woman's history cannot grow.

Black Foremothers: Three Lives is a part of the phenomenal social revolution taking place now in women's affairs. These factual narratives further elaborate on the options open to women: wage-earner? homemaker? combination of both? The many stringent restrictions on American women have always been trebled for black women because of race and class as well as sex. The lives of these three black women illustrate how women have historically dealt with problems of discrimination, injustice, and social ostracism for a very long time in American society.

More than a century has passed since chattel slavery was ended by law and by war in these United States of America. The fight for human rights, however, has continued. The entire Third World has marshaled militant forces for freedom of black, brown, yellow, and red people in this hemisphere and, indeed, all over the earth. The women's movement has been a parallel struggle for freedom, peace, and human dignity. Even in pre-Civil War days, black women stood in the vanguard for equal rights; for freedom from slavery, for recognition of women as citizens and co-partners with men in all of life's endeavors. Harriet Tubman and Sojourner Truth were among the earliest of black women leaders who participated in both the abolitionist movement and the women's struggle. Sojourner's famous "And aren't I a woman?" speech is often quoted as an example of her spirited and active engagement in the women's movement. Frances Watkins Harper, an antebellum black woman, an educated poet and novelist, worked as hard for women's rights and temperance as she worked for the abolition of slavery.

However, because of the nature of American history, and particularly because of the institutions of slavery and segregation, the names and lives of black women leaders are all but unknown in American society—black as well as white. The names of a handful of black women leaders of the past may be familiar—Harriet Tubman, Sojourner Truth, Mary McCleod Bethune are perhaps among the best-known. The names and accomplishments of recent civil rights leaders—Fannie Lou Hamer of Mississippi, Daisy Bates of Arkansas, Gloria Richardson of Tidewater country in Maryland and Virginia—have scarcely reached the ears of American schoolchildren. The few contemporary leaders who are widely recognized, such as Shirley Chisholm and Barbara Jordan, are viewed as unique, having nothing whatever in common with the mass of black women and their history in this country.

This book recovers from history three great black American women, women who were fighters for freedom—freedom from slavery of the mind and the spirit as well as freedom of the body from the despicable use of a human being as a piece of property or a thing. All three women—Ellen Craft, Ida B. Wells, Mary Church Terrell—were born in the nineteenth century. All three were women of great beauty, character, and ability. Although their circumstances were very different—Ellen Craft growing up as an unlettered slave, Ida Wells scrimping pennies for an education, Mary Church Terrell the daughter of the South's first black millionaire—they were equally indomitable and courageous. Every woman, man, and child should know their stories and the significance of their achievements and experiences. Taken together, these *Three Lives* span one hundred and twenty-eight years—from 1826, the year of Ellen Craft's birth, to 1954, the year of Mary Church Terrell's death. Because of the diverse interests of these women, the major social and political upheavals of the period—from the slavery controversies of the 1850s to the McCarthy witch hunts of the 1950s—move through these pages.

The lives of the women overlap in interesting and crucial ways: some of the antislavery leaders who welcomed Ellen Craft to England in the mid-nineteenth century were inspired to form antilynching societies upon Ida Wells's English lecture tour forty-five years later. A Mississippi Valley yellow fever epidemic took the lives of Ida Wells's parents and brought her happy childhood to an agonizingly abrupt end; a second epidemic, one year later, led Mary Church's father to the great fortune that turned her privileged childhood into an even more privileged young womanhood. Mary Church Terrell's kind of integrity kept her in the National Association for the Advancement of Colored People, which she and Wells helped to found in 1909—while Ida Wells's kind of integrity very shortly drove her out of it. Both women were associates of Ellen Craft's daughter, Ellen Craft Crum, in the earliest days of organizing black women into a national association. There are countless other connections, both private and historic.

The multiple interests and activities of Craft, Wells, and Terrell that you will read about in the following pages are a reflection of concerns that have been common to black women, who have been active on every social and political front, from the days of chattel slavery to the present. What is far from typical, however, is the relative freedom of all three women from the grinding poverty and ceaseless drudgery of the mass of black women. Released—although in varying degrees—from the daily struggle for mere survival, Craft, Wells, and Terrell were able to devote more of themselves to social and political causes than were the vast majority of their sisters.

Although these three women all faced challenges and problems because of their sex, their first great obstacle was racism. Advantaged as they were, their stories make clear that none of them was spared the disappointments, griefs, humiliations of racial prejudice and hatred. But this trio of black heroes shared a sturdy ability to rise above disappointment, to rebound even from disaster. That ability—what would be called today an important "survival trait"—was not the only thing they had in common. All three possessed a self-confidence that enabled them to dare to exercise their gifts of intellect and leadership, during times when women—to say nothing of women who were black—were not encouraged to do so. All three wandered far from their native South, not only traveling widely in their own country, but crossing and recrossing oceans, even dwelling in foreign lands. Of the three, only Ellen Craft finally returned to her origins, to rural Georgia.

Ellen Craft became a legend in her own time because of her daring escape from slavery. Dorothy Sterling's biography of her is a remarkable achievement. The first full-length separate account we have ever had of Ellen Craft's life, it is the first to give her her due, bringing her out from behind the shadow of her husband, William—a feat which required painstaking research, finally yielding us an exciting new view of this intrepid, kindly, winning woman. Disguised as a man and posing as her husband's young white master, Ellen Craft made her escape from Georgia, arriving safely with William on free soil, after many perilous adventures. The story did not, of course, end there; and women of today will find inspiration in the story of Ellen's development from an illiterate servant to a great woman who became the servant of a great movement, a teacher of her people, and a protector of the poor, the weak, and the helpless.

A public housing project stands today in the city of Chicago as a monument to Ida B. Wells. A native Mississippian, she became a national leader among black people, the first to bring to international attention the unspeakable crime of lynching. Educated first at Rust College in Holly Springs, Mississippi, later at Fisk University and Lemoyne Institute, at sixteen she became a teacher in order to support her orphaned sisters and brothers. But it was journalism that offered Ida Wells scope not only for her writing abilities, but for her dawning commitment to the advancement of her people. Ida Wells was a bold and tireless "investigative reporter" long before that term was coined. Nothing could stop her in her struggle against racism, sexism, and the violent crime of lynching. A married woman and a mother, a writer, a lecturer, an unpaid social worker among Chicago's poor and dispossessed, Ida Wells set an example of high moral integrity and principled virtue for all her sisters in America, white as well as black.

I was fortunate enough to meet personally the third of this trio of great American women of my race. Mary Church Terrell was a strong, beautiful, forceful, and intelligent fighter for freedom, even into her eighth decade of life. When I saw her, I was impressed with the enduring keenness of her intellect and her passion for justice, but most impressive was the moral strength she communicated. Dorothy Sterling has captured this moral fiber in her portrait of stooped, white-haired Mrs. Terrell, impeccably groomed, leading a civil rights picket line "with a cane in one hand and a picket sign in the other . . . during December snowstorms and the sweltering days of summer." The most fortunate of these three women, if fortune can be measured in terms of economic opportunities and social advantages, she was the most cosmopolitan, and probably the most erudite. She leaves as her monument and personal testament a book about women—about what it means to be a black woman in America—*A Colored Woman in a*

White World. Terrell fought unequivocally for racial equality, for civil rights legislation, against lynch law, against cold war hysteria; she was especially active in the national organizing of black women. Interested in every civic endeavor of her time, she was the first black woman to serve on the board of education in the nation's capital. As a suffragist and peace activist, she represented black women abroad in meetings in Germany, Switzerland, and England. Receiving honorary degrees from many universities, she was named one of the hundred most distinguished alumni of Oberlin College.

Early in this century, the women's fight in America was for the ballot. Suffragists marched and suffered and won the battle. But it was only one battle in an ongoing war. Women of all races and strata of society have enlisted in this struggle for human rights. For it is more than a fight for women, it is a fight for all human beings. Black women, as always, are caught up in the crisis of more than one struggle. We have an ongoing struggle for the rights of black people, and we have never lost sight of the fact that we are women, exploited as much as because of our sex as because of our race and our poverty.

Black women have found themselves in a peculiar position in the women's movement from its inception. No women in the world have been treated more like pariahs than black women. We have been exploited as sex objects, made to suffer the galling attacks of men of all races, cruelly put upon because of our sex, economic station, and race. Yet there has always been a strange dichotomy even in the women's movement; and here the black abolitionists, suffragists, and feminist workers have all met with the same problem. When the time came to take a stand, white women and black women parted company over race. In the suffrage movement, northern white feminists were afraid to offend their white southern sisters. Ida B. Wells was told, on one occasion, not to join a Washington, D.C. suffrage demonstration, "lest her dark-skinned presence antagonize" white southern women. (Typically, the irrepressible Ida B., "marched anyway," as Dorothy Sterling tells us.) Even the greatest of white women leaders regarded sex as more important than race and claimed that race must take second place. For black women this was untenable; and they said so. Wells and Terrell each fought within the women's movement for the recognition that black women must have the ballot and equal consideration in all matters of importance to women.

There are now overwhelming social factors at work in our society. The women's movement must come of age, as must all struggles for the rights of human beings. Racism and sexism alike must go. They belong equally to the past. They have no place in a future that can only be founded on a new world order of international understanding, cultural pluralism, full human rights.

In these simple and lucid biographies, Dorothy Sterling has represented a trio of black women with unusual faithfulness and understanding. Each woman is etched against her time and place in American life. Each of these women came to occupy a station of honor, pride, and achievement. Independent in disposition, but devoted to home and family, and above all to her race and gender, each left the mark of her presence on American society.

The publication of Stein's *Three Lives* in 1909 was an auspicious event, not only because the black woman Melanctha held the center of the stage, but because instead of a fictional Negro female stereotype, Stein gave us a fully drawn human being. Now Dorothy Sterling and The Feminist Press have given us three stories of real-life black heroes. If these women loom larger than life, that is because we have not understood how many other brave black women went before us. Many of them are lost to us forever; but many of their histories can be recovered, to take their places alongside the lives of Ellen Craft, Ida B. Wells, and Mary Church Terrell.

From the exigencies of slavery, poverty, ignorance, and expressions of violent white racism, these three black women are successfully lifted before the eyes of the world. This, too, is an auspicious event. Let us hope that it is a new beginning.

MARGARET WALKER

Publisher's Preface

THE EIGHT YEARS since the first edition of *Black Foremothers* was published have been a period of achievement as well as continued struggle for black women in the United States. Historical scholarship by and about black women has been an area of advancement, with black female historians publishing in ever-growing numbers and gaining greater recognition for their work, and with black women's history included to a greater extent as a topic of scholarship. The recent work of scholars such as Paula Giddings, Jacqueline Jones, Bettina Aptheker, Marianna Davis, James Oliver Horton, Joanne V. Hawks, Sheila L. Skemp, Dolores E. Janiewski, Lois Acharf, Joan M. Jensen, Angela Davis, Bell Hooks, Darlene Hines, Dorothy Sterling, Deborah White, Jean Fagan Yellin, Nell Irvin Painter, Marilyn Richardson, Gloria Hull, and Minrose Gwin are examples of the importance of black women's history and voices in current scholarship.

Ellen Craft, Ida B. Wells, and Mary Church Terrell figure directly in the work of some of these scholars, and they are important, furthermore, because their own work was an integral part of the struggles of 1826 to 1954 which advanced race and sex equality and laid the foundation for the work which continues to this day. For eight years *Black Foremothers* has made their stories—thoroughly researched and engagingly told—available to students, teachers, and the general reader. This new edition provides a comprehensive introduction by Barbara Christian not available in the previous edition. The introduction provides historical context for each woman's life and incorporates insights into how we can view these lives gleaned from the new scholarship that has been written in the past few years.

Publisher's Acknowledgments

EARLY IN 1973, Mariam Chamberlain and Terry Saario of the Ford Foundation spent one day visiting The Feminist Press on the campus of the State University of New York, College at Old Westbury. They heard staff members describe the early history of The Feminist Press and its goal—to change the sexist education of girls and boys, women and men, through publishing and other projects. They also heard about those books and projects then in progress; they felt our sense of frustration about how little we were able to do directly for the classroom teacher. Advising us about funding, Terry Saario was provocative. "You need to think of yourselves," she said, "in the manner of language labs, testing and developing new texts for students and new instructional materials for teachers." Our "language" was feminism, our intent to provide alternatives to the sexist texts used in schools. The conception was, in fact, precisely the one on which the Press had been founded.

Out of that 1973 meeting came the idea for the *Women's Lives/ Women's Work* project. This project, which would not officially begin for more than two years, has allowed us to extend the original concept of The Feminist Press to a broader audience.

In the summer of 1975, the final proposal—to produce for co-publication a series of twelve supplementary books and their accompanying teaching guides—was funded by the Ford Foundation and the Carnegie Corporation. Project officers Terry Saario and Vivien Stewart were supportive and helpful throughout the life of the project.

Once funding was obtained, The Feminist Press began its search for additional staff to work on the project. The small nucleus of existing staff working on the project was expanded as The Feminist Press hired new employees. The *Women's Lives/Women's Work* project staff ultimately included eight people who remained for the duration of the project: Sue Davidson, Shirley Frank, Merle Froschl, Florence Howe, Mary Mulrooney, Elizabeth Phillips, Susan Trowbridge, and Sandy Weinbaum. Two other people, Dora Janeway Odarenko and Michele Russell, were on the staff through 1977, and we wish to acknowledge their contributions. Helen Schrader, a Feminist Press staff member, participated on the project during its first year and kept financial records and wrote financial reports throughout the duration of the project.

The *Women's Lives/Women's Work* project staff adopted the methods of work and the decision-making structure developed by

The Feminist Press staff as a whole. As a Press "work committee," the project met weekly to make decisions, review progress, discuss problems. The project staff refined the editorial direction of the project, conceptualized and devised guidelines for the books, and identified prospective authors. When proposals came in, the project staff read and evaluated the submissions, and made decisions regarding them. Similarly, when manuscripts arrived, the project staff read and commented on them. Project staff members took turns drafting memoranda, reports, and other documents. And the design of the series grew out of the discussions and the ideas generated at the project meetings. The books, teaching guides, and other informational materials had the advantage, at significant stages of development, of the committee's collective direction.

The process of evaluation by teachers and students before final publication was as important as the process for developing ideas into books. To this end, we produced testing editions of the books. Field-testing networks were set up throughout the United States in a variety of schools—public, private, inner-city, small town, suburban, and rural—to reach as diverse a student population as possible. We field tested in the following cities, regions, and states: Boston, Massachusetts; Tucson, Arizona; Seattle, Washington; Los Angeles, California; Tampa, Florida; Greensboro, North Carolina; Eugene, Oregon; Martha's Vineyard, Massachusetts; New York City; Long Island; New Jersey; Rhode Island. We also had an extensive network of educators—350 teachers across the country—who reviewed the books in the series, often using sections of books in classrooms. From teachers' comments, from students' questionnaires, and from tapes of teachers' discussions, we gained valuable information both for revising the books and for developing the teaching guides.

Although there is no easy way to acknowledge the devotion and enthusiasm of hundreds of teachers who willingly volunteered their time and energies, we would like to thank the following teachers— and their students—with whom we worked directly in the testing of *Black Foremothers: Three Lives*. In New York City: Elyse Aronauer, Lynn Kearney, Roberta Kronberger, Mary McAulay, Karen Mackey, Susan Metz, Marlane Nussbaum. In North Carolina, Sandra Powers, professor of education at the University of North Carolina/Greensboro—with the assistance of Anita Hawkins—helped to contact teachers in and near Greensboro: Joanie Anderson, Mary Anderson, Marilyn Z. Cotten, Patricia L. Gottlieb, J. P. Hendrix, Annie N. Thompson. In Florida, Mary Bullerman, director of Instructional Services for the Hillsborough County School System, and Ellen Kimmel, professor of education at the University of South Florida/Tampa, helped to contact teachers in the Tampa Bay area: Gayl E. Davis, Edie Edwards, Miriam Katz, Sylvia Lampert, Pam Livingston, Sara Kate Milledge, Katie Sible, Catherine A. Steinker. We would also like to acknowledge the participation of Eloise M. Fells of the Federal Sex Desegregation Center at the University of Miami.

Three times during the life of the *Women's Lives/Women's Work* project, an Advisory Board composed of feminist educators and scholars met for a full day to discuss the books and teaching guides. The valuable criticisms and suggestions of the following people who participated in these meetings were essential to the project: Millie Alpern, Rosalynn Baxandall, Peggy Brick, Ellen Cantarow, Elizabeth Ewen, Barbara Gates, Clarisse Gillcrist, Elaine Hedges, Nancy Hoffman, Susan Klaw, Alice Kessler-Harris, Roberta Kronberger, Merle Levine, Eleanor Newirth, Judith Oksner, Naomi Rosenthal, Judith Schwartz, Judy Scott, Carroll Smith-Rosenberg, Adria Steinberg, Barbara Sussman, Amy Swerdlow. We also want to express our gratitude to Shirley McCune and Nida Thomas, who acted in a general advisory capacity and made many useful suggestions; and to Kathryn Girard and Kathy Salisbury, who helped to develop the teacher and student field-testing questionnaires.

In particular we want to thank Flavia Rando, whose exhaustive photo research and unbounded perseverance enabled us to portray Craft, Wells, Terrell, and their contemporaries in photo features as well as in prose. And we wish to acknowledge Ruth Adam for restoration of the historical photographs; Judith H. McQuown, who prepared the index; Hester Eggert and Carlos Ruiz of McGraw-Hill for administrative assistance; Emerson W. Madairy and Linda Petillo of Monotype Composition Company for technical assistance; and Elaine Scott, of State University of New York at Old Westbury, who helped us to make choices among signal events in black history for the historical table.

The assistance of the many people mentioned in these acknowledgments has been invaluable to us. We would also like to thank all of you who will read this book—because you helped to create the demand that made the *Women's Lives/Women's Work* project possible.

Author's Acknowledgments

MY GREATEST DEBT is to Alfreda Duster, daughter of Ida Wells and editor of her autobiography, *Crusade for Justice.* In lengthy interviews and in reply to innumerable queries, she gave me a well-rounded picture of the life and personality of her mother. Phyllis Terrell Langston recalled several illuminating anecdotes about her mother, and was kind enough to lend me three of Mary Church Terrell's diaries. Annie Stein, who had been executive secretary of the Coordinating Committee for the Enforcement of the D. C. Anti-Discrimination Laws, was particularly illuminating about Mrs. Terrell in the last years of her life. Dorothy Porter, former curator of the Moorland-Spingarn Research Center at Howard University, not only reminisced about Mrs. Terrell, whose papers she had helped to assemble, but went through her own voluminous files to locate a number of references to Ellen Craft. The Reverend Albert Foley of Spring Hill College, Mobile, Alabama, biographer of Ellen Craft's nephew, Bishop James A. Healy, generously sent me a considerable body of information on Craft's father, on her second master, and on the families of both men. Letters from Julia Craft De Costa, Ellen Craft's granddaughter; Samuel L. Akers, former dean of Wesleyan College; and the Reverend Cannon A. R. Winnett of Ockham, England, were also helpful.

DOROTHY STERLING

Introduction

THE HISTORY OF BLACK WOMEN has been neglected because they are members of two social groups—women and blacks—who traditionally have been ignored by historians. And, as a glance at history texts will suggest, the resurgence of interest in women's history and black history that began at the end of the sixties has not led to the inclusion of black women in most texts or the history curriculum. When black women are mentioned in those texts, they are portrayed as passive victims of slavery or racial oppression, rather than as active participants in American life.

Since most historians have not recognized the experience of black women as significant, primary sources still need to be discovered, compiled, and organized. Even the papers of prominent black women such as Ida B. Wells or Mary McLeod Bethune are scattered in libraries, never having been edited. Biographies of black women, therefore, are scarce; those that exist are about women for whom there is readily available information. Recently, however, a number of scholars have begun to research the lives of black women, and to interpret the rich store of existing documents and oral traditions. *Black Foremothers* is part of this ongoing effort to research, preserve, and write the history of black women.

Black Foremothers chronicles the lives of three extraordinary women: Ellen Craft, Ida B. Wells, and Mary Church Terrell. They were extraordinary in their courageous stands against racism and sexism, in their departure from conventional societal norms for women of their period, in their intelligence, and in their leadership qualities. These dynamic and successful women dedicated their lives to seeking social justice for black people and to working for sexual equality. At a time when it was uncommon for married women to work outside the home, they combined motherhood with life-long careers of political organizing, community service, writing, and lecturing. Although the achievements of these women are outstanding, many aspects of their lives are typical of the lives of other black women who were their contemporaries. The fact that they were light-skinned and, in the case of Terrell and Wells, part of an educated black elite, did not protect them from racial discrimination. The problems of coping with racist slurs, finding decent medical care, traveling in the Jim Crow South, working with whites in political organizations, or applying for jobs in the government linked their lives to all blacks of their day—whatever their social class or educational background.

As slaves or the children of slaves, the legacy of their bondage shaped their lives. It was this legacy that inspired their intense concern for the integrity and cohesion of their families. The problems that they faced as mothers in raising their children both to survive in a racist society and to resist discrimination typified the experiences of all black mothers. Their drive for education—and the use they made of this education to assist black communities—linked them with many educated black women of their day.

These three biographies also illuminate several other neglected aspects of black history. From Reconstruction on, black women organized to provide services that the government and white social welfare organizations failed to supply. These institutions included clinics, schools, day nurseries, homes for the aged, and cultural centers. The story of this work accomplished by thousands of black club women throughout the country is rarely told. Similarly absent from history is the story of black feminism. It often has been assumed that black women have not been feminists because historically they have given primary emphasis to the struggle for racial equality. But there is a strong tradition of black feminism epitomized by women such as Ida B. Wells and Mary Church Terrell. They flaunted prescribed roles for wives and mothers and supported a wide range of feminist issues. Indeed, as Dorothy Sterling's biographies show, such black women lived feminist lives in spite of the racism they encountered in the suffrage and women's club movements. An understanding of their feminism is essential to an understanding of the black feminist movement today.

Black Foremothers also contributes to an understanding of the work of black women in movements for social change of the nineteenth and twentieth centuries. All three women made significant contributions to one or more of these major movements—abolitionism, the struggle against lynching and Jim Crow laws, women's suffrage.

In short, *Black Foremothers* can be used to learn about three outstanding black women who rarely are mentioned in history texts. Their biographies explore the contributions of black women to social movements and the major black political organizations of their day. In addition, their lives shed light on the concerns of all black women who were their contemporaries.

Black Foremothers also provides insights into black literature and biography—specifically about problems in writing the biographies of black women. Often black women have been denied education and, therefore, have left few written records. For example, Dorothy Sterling had to reconstruct Ellen Craft's life largely from the writings of contemporaries—many of them white—and from William Craft's account of their escape. To write about Ellen Craft's fears and hopes, Sterling often had to rely on imaginative reconstructions of emotions and reactions. Wells's and Terrell's lives, on the other hand, are well documented. They both left voluminous correspondence as well as private diaries and published autobiographies.

Ellen Craft

Slave women were essential to the economy of the antebellum South. As field hands, they worked alongside men from dawn to sunset hoeing; building fences; cutting down trees; constructing dikes; pulling fodder; clearing land; planting tobacco, cotton, rice, sugar, and corn; and then harvesting the crop. Those women who did not work in the fields were domestic servants. They worked in the houses of their owners cooking and serving meals, tending gardens, caring for livestock and chickens, sewing clothes, carding and spinning wool, cleaning, churning butter, running errands, waiting on their masters and mistresses, and nursing and tending the owners' children. Slave women were valued not only for their work, but also for their fertility. After the slave trade was outlawed, slave owners depended on the reproductive capacities of their slaves to make the slave economy possible. Slaves could only live together with the permission of their owners (marriages were not recognized legally although many slaves did in fact have "marriage" ceremonies), and the owners placed high value on a woman in good health who would be likely to bear many children.

The experiences of slave women varied depending on the type of work they did, on the size of the plantation on which they lived, and on their owners. On large plantations, such as the Smith's, the work of slaves was likely to be more specialized and less closely supervised than the work of slaves on small farms. Large plantations included slaves who were skilled artisans, such as Ellen and William Craft. In general, house slaves and skilled artisans lived better than field slaves; they usually had better clothes and food; they had greater access to information and, in some cases, were able to learn to read and write in spite of the legal prohibition against teaching slaves. House slaves, however, had the disadvantage of being at the beck and call of their masters and mistresses and of constantly being under their supervision. Slaves, such as the Crafts, who hired themselves out in town—an option open to a minority of slaves—had, of course, the greatest access to information about the outside world and the greatest possibilities for escape.

As historian Jacqueline Jones demonstrates, the persistence with which slaves sought to define, on their own terms, what a woman should be would ultimately have a profound effect on Afro-American history. Although slave masters ignored gender conventions about what work slave women and men did, the slave community constructed its own division of labor within households. If necessary, slave men cooked, sewed, and took care of children. However, while these tasks were highly valued for survival, they were usually considered women's work. Slave women on large plantations, as in the case of Ellen Craft, were especially valued for home textile production—spinning, weaving, sewing. Gender conventions about the work slaves did was affected by the tension between slave masters' demands and the needs and desires of slave households.

Whatever work slave women did, they, like the men, were subject to the overseer's lash for any infraction of discipline. While not all masters beat their slaves, slave narratives testify to the many who did and to other forms of sadistic punishment. Pregnant women reported having to dig holes for their bellies so that they could lie down to receive their flogging. All slave women also lived under the constant threat of rape. Rape was not a peripheral aspect of plantation life; it was central to the arsenal of weapons that owners had at their command to control slaves. Slave masters perceived slave women as sexual objects due to the popular belief that they were hot-blooded wenches, in contrast to the virtuous southern lady. This myth was one means by which southern society justified the rape of women. Women hesitated to resist because of the threat of separation from their families and harm to their children; and black men were helpless to prevent the sexual abuse of their mothers, wives, sisters, and lovers. Mulatto children were in some cases favored by their owners, but in many cases were subject to the particular wrath of the mistress who herself felt powerless to protest her humiliation in a system in which white men controlled all women and children—both black and white.

The greatest threat that slaves faced was separation from their families. According to conservative estimates, 32.4 percent of slave families were separated by their owners.* Even after separation, however, slaves were able to maintain the integrity of their family life—

---

*John W. Blassingame, *The Slave Community: Plantation Life in the Ante-Bellum South* (New York: Oxford University Press, 1972), p. 91.

they kept contact with relatives on other plantations, risked their lives to visit and to smuggle messages to their children or spouses, and in some cases they worked to buy the freedom of their children. Women kept the children of friends and kin, thus providing continuity in family relationships. Since women were at the core of the extended family system, they were especially responsible for keeping alive the sense of family. In a world that offered few satisfactions, family life that was not under the direct supervision and control of the slave owner was valued above all else.

Whether house or field slave, most slave women did not live in situations that allowed many chances for escape. It has been estimated by historians that the majority of runaway slaves were young men between the ages of sixteen and thirty. Because slave women tended to have children at an early age, they were less likely to attempt escape. Obviously, it was very difficult to evade the patrols that roamed the countryside if one was traveling with children, and few slave women would leave their children behind. A few did manage to runaway with children in their arms, but the women noted for successful escapes, such as Harriet Tubman or Ellen Craft, did not have children.

However, slave women resisted slavery in other overt ways. Some mammies poisoned their masters, an act that panicked slaveholders above all else; others sabotaged work, stole food, burned buildings, or fed runaway slaves. A few participated in the establishment of maroons—settlements of fugitive slaves who successfully evaded their captors, sometimes for many years.

The most pervasive acts of resistance, however, were more covert and persistent ones. Slave women daily practiced acts of survival as a means of resisting the brutal physical and psychological impact of slavery. They taught their children to survive as slaves while preserving and encouraging their self-respect. Through religion, storytelling, and song, they passed on characteristics of black culture that helped to keep their people strong. Slave narratives testify to the strength slave women exhibited in resisting the degradation of slavery, in maintaining their fervent belief that they had a right to be free, and in sustaining the hope for freedom in their children. Their persistent belief in their own humanity undercut the most basic principle of slavery—that blacks were less than human.

As early as 1775, a few white male Americans had proclaimed publicly that they wished to put an end to slavery when they founded the Pennsylvania Society for Promoting the Abolition of Slavery.

Similar groups developed in the late eighteenth century, both in the North and the South. However, most of these early abolitionists were gradualists who believed that slavery would come to a natural end, that Southerners should be compensated for their loss of slaves, and that blacks should be sent away from America and colonized. Free blacks were not allowed into these societies, for the early abolitionists wished to wipe away the national sin of slavery, rather than declaring blacks as equal to whites.

The militant, mainly Northern, abolitionist movement began in the 1830s. This movement was distinguished initially by the intense participation of free black men and women who originally had organized in the 1820s to oppose the idea of the colonization of American blacks. These black men and women joined with the Boston reformer, William Lloyd Garrison, as well as with other concerned whites, to work for the immediate abolition of slavery. The first step in this battle was the formation of the American Anti-Slavery Society (AASS) in December 1833.

The new abolitionism also was characterized by the organization of women's auxiliaries, an innovative and progressive step for that time. Less than a month after the founding of the AASS, the Female Anti-Slavery Society of Philadelphia was formed. At this meeting, a black Quaker, Sarah Douglass, invited the Grimké sisters, Angelina and Sarah, to speak on slavery and women's rights. Four black women were founders of that group: Sarah Douglass, Harriet Purvis, and Sarah and Margaretta Forten. These, as well as many other black women, helped to organize the new abolitionist thrust. Though few historians note it, black women were active in the abolitionist movement from its beginnings and helped to formulate its major concepts and strategies.

The major principle of abolitionism was that slavery in the United States should be abolished immediately. Along with this fundamental principle, the dominant Garrison faction asserted that *blacks* and *women* should have the same rights as white men. This position, however, was not put into practice by most white abolitionists. Black men and women protested race prejudice within the movement itself, as well as the ambivalence among white abolitionists on the question of the vote for free blacks in the North. And some white women who protested their treatment in the movement practiced racial discrimination against their black sisters. In 1835, black women who sought membership in the Massachusetts Female Anti-Slavery Society at Fall River caused such consternation among its white members that the group almost fell apart. Later, the issue was raised of admitting black delegates to the first two national female antislavery conventions in 1837 and 1838. Sarah Forten, one of the black delegates who finally was admitted, circulated a poem calling upon white women to abandon race prejudice. As a result of such incidents, black women formed their own societies.

Black abolitionists were interested not only in turning the tide of public sentiment against slavery, but also in freeing as many slaves as possible. To that end, they helped to organize the Underground Railroad and the committees that helped runaway slaves when they reached "Freedom Land." Harriet Tubman, an escaped slave, was the most famous person of the Underground Railroad; she conducted hundreds of slaves from South to North. As important as her work were the fundraising and organizing drives of innumerable black women who helped to provide money for the Railroad and who aided runaway slaves in finding jobs in the North. Whites were often not attuned to the survival concerns of escaped slaves, so that free blacks found themselves responsible for the adaptation of ex-slaves to their new home.

In addition to antislavery work, black women participated actively in the struggle for equal rights for blacks. Their primary goal was to organize educational facilities such as libraries and schools for free blacks; to work in the self-help programs, such as the temperance societies that blacks organized to rid the free black community of alcoholism; and to campaign for the vote for blacks in the North. Frances Ellen Watkins Harper is especially noteworthy for her activism in these areas.

Abolitionist activities reached a peak after the passage of the Fugitive Slave Law of 1850, which mandated the return of runaway slaves found in the North to their "rightful owner." As a result of this legislation, some blacks began to advocate emigration—at least as a temporary expedient. In the three months following the passage of the Fugitive Slave Law, some three hundred blacks fled to Canada; in the ten years after 1850, the numbers reached fifteen thousand. Mary Ann Shadd was the chief proponent of Canadian emigration. Through her paper, *The Provincial Freeman*, and numerous lecture tours, she was able to promote her views. Though some black abolitionists, like Shadd, supported emigration for blacks, the majority opposed this view and concentrated on demonstrating against the Fugitive Slave Law.

As the abolitionist movement developed, its most important tactic became the lectures given at meetings throughout the North. The most effective lectures were given by ex-slaves, such as the Crafts.

Not only were these lectures emotionally compelling, but they also served to illustrate the intelligence and humanity of slaves to an audience that needed proof. Black men like Frederick Douglass, Henry Bibb, and William Wells Brown became famous for their witnessing. And increasingly, female ex-slaves, such as Harriet Tubman, Sojourner Truth, and Ellen Craft began to speak in public, for only they could communicate the experience of female slaves. Spurred on by the impact their sisters made, free black women such as Frances Ellen Watkins Harper, Mary Ann Shadd, and Sarah Remond would speak not only to black audiences, as they had done previously, but to white abolitionist meetings and conferences. After the passage of the Fugitive Slave Law, Ellen Craft and Sarah Remond promoted abolitionism in England. This international aspect was important, for England supported the North when the Civil War began.

One effect of the abolitionist lectures was the introduction, in general, of American women to the podium. Nineteenth-century American society did not approve of women speaking in public; it was believed that women should remain at home caring for husbands and children, while men earned wages, fought wars, and governed. The first woman to speak publicly in abolitionist meetings was a black woman, Maria Stewart, who did so in 1832 with a profound awareness of the outrageous quality of her action. She was followed by many other women—both black and white—although not without considerable opposition from many male leaders.

Although free black women and runaway slave women were prominent actors in the abolitionist movement, men played the central roles in black northern institutions. Black newspapers of the time exhorted black women to be "true women," and to defer to black men since white society sought to emasculate them. Black women did protest these restrictions. For example, historian James Horton reports that at the 1849 Ohio State meeting of blacks, "black ladies threatened to walk out and never return if they were not allowed to take part in the discussion."

As abolitionist women learned political skills and gained confidence in their organizing and speaking abilities, they began to resent the limitations placed on their access to public forums and the lack of equality between women and men in the leadership of the abolitionist movement. Indeed, the women's movement eventually developed from the discontent of white and black women over the roles prescribed for them within the abolitionist organizations. The more confident they became, the more clearly they saw the parallels between their own inferior status as women and that of slaves.

Beginning in 1848, women formed their own organizations to struggle for women's legal, political, and economic rights. Black abolitionists such as Sojourner Truth, Harriet Tubman, and Frederick Douglass participated actively in the women's movement from its inception; however, racial tensions flared as they had earlier in abolitionist organizations when some white women attempted to exclude blacks from speaking at the women's rights conventions. These tensions and conflicts over racial issues continued to surface in the women's rights movement throughout its nineteenth- and early twentieth-century history.

Immediately after the end of the Civil War, whites in the South attempted to reverse some of their losses by enacting Black Codes, whose purpose was to return blacks to a state of virtual slavery. The Black Codes limited the kinds of jobs blacks could hold, thereby forcing them to work for whites for low wages or as sharecroppers for their former masters. The codes also restricted blacks' freedom of movement. To enforce these codes, white protective societies, such as the Ku Klux Klan and Camellias, roamed the countryside threatening and punishing blacks who refused to conform.

The result of the South's resistance to freeing blacks was the passage by Congress of the Reconstruction Act of 1867. It declared the existing southern regimes illegal and established five military districts in the South that were to prepare their provinces for readmission to the Union. A distinguishing feature of the Reconstruction Act was its requirement that black males be given the vote.

For many white Southerners, the Reconstruction Act was graphic evidence of the North's victory over them, and they turned their anger and hostility against blacks. In addition to legislative acts and physical violence against blacks, slandering of any successful black, such as William Craft, was not uncommon.

Like the Crafts, many blacks who had had the opportunity to become educated entered the Reconstruction period with a deep sense of responsibility for the "uplifting" of their race. These blacks focused their energy particularly on education, for most ex-slaves were unable to read and write. The Freedmen's Bureau, a Federal agency entrusted with the welfare of the free blacks after the war, made its greatest achievement in the area of education. The Bureau taught more than one-quarter million black children in its five-year history; its four thousand schools became the foundation for the public school system in the South. After 1870, when the Freedmen's Bureau was abolished, the number of black women teachers increased rapidly as educated black women staffed or founded schools of their own. Even before the abolition of slavery, black women clandestinely had operated schools both in the South and in the North; Mary S. Peake, a seamstress from Hampton, Virginia; Sarah Douglass, the Quaker abolitionist; Charlotte Forten, a free Northern black, who was one of the first to volunteer to teach in the schools established by the Freedmen's Bureau. Ellen Craft's decision to found a school was part of this movement in education spearheaded by black women.

Black educators of the Reconstruction South were characterized by a missionary zeal to "uplift" their race. Since most female exslaves had worked primarily in the fields and had scarcely a home to call their own, a major aim of black educators was to teach these women domestic skills. Black schools stressed home economics as well as a rigid code of behavior, and teachers often presented the role of wife and mother as the highest goal a women could achieve.

Black women's major concern after the close of the Civil War was to escape economic hardship while keeping their families intact. If they could, they sought to housekeep rather than enter the wage labor market, a tendency that whites resented. While white women were expected to stay at home, black women were condemned by whites if they "played the lady." At the same time, black women were not able, as black men were, to enter the male-dominated area of politics. Black women enjoyed neither the male privileges nor female "rewards" of the day.

The lives of most black women during Reconstruction and afterward had little to do with the nineteenth-century ideal of womanhood. Black women sharecropped, worked in tobacco factories, and toiled in domestic service. Only a few, like Ellen Craft, owned their own farms. In her series of essays, *Black Women in the Reconstruction South*, Frances Ellen Watkins Harper documents how even well-off black women did "double duty, a man's share in the field, even ploughing and at home the cooking, washing, milking, and gardening." In addition, these women felt responsible for their communities and provided charitable services, as well as health care and education. They were usually personally responsible for the extended family, and for the care of the elderly as well as the indigent. By the 1880s, many of these women, like Ellen Craft, saw their hard work undermined by an intense resurgence of white supremacy in the South. In spite of these reversals, however, they helped to end slavery in America and to create a world in which their children, no longer slaves, could continue to fight for equality.

Ida B. Wells

In 1876, the Republican presidential candidate, Rutherford B. Hayes, almost lost the election to his Democratic opponent, Samuel J. Tilden because of disputed results from several Southern states. A specially selected Electoral Commission was chosen and decided the election in Hayes's favor. He promised to placate the South by withdrawing federal troops. When the last vestige of protection for blacks was withdrawn, the remaining Republican governments were quickly dismantled, and the political repression and terror against blacks that had characterized the immediate post-Civil War period was resumed. Ida B. Wells described the three prongs of this offensive in her pamphlet *Red Record:* the violent suppression of so-called "race riots"; laws disenfranchising black men, and lynching ostensibly for the rape of white women. The "race riots" characterized the period immediately after the war. In 1866 in Memphis, a race riot was used by whites as the justification for acts of violence and the destruction of black property. Forty-six blacks were killed, seventy wounded, and more than a dozen black schools and churches burned. A similar toll was taken on the black community of New Orleans in the same year.

Throughout Reconstruction, blacks had been intimidated from voting through acts of physical violence and terror committed by the Ku Klux Klan and other vigilante groups. However, beginning in 1890, Mississippi led the way in officially disenfranchising blacks in the state constitution. Laws were passed requiring voters to pay a poll tax, pass a literacy test involving interpretation of the state constitution, and pass a character test. To insure that poor uneducated whites would not be caught in the dragnet of these laws, "grandfather" clauses were passed in some states assuring the vote to those whose grandfathers had voted in January 1867, when blacks did not yet have the vote.

The third means of repression was lynching, often for the unproven crime of rape of a white woman. In 1894, Wells reported that the number of persons put to death through lynching—ninety percent of them black—exceeded the number who were executed by law.

The political repression was upheld by a judicial system that disqualified blacks from sitting on juries and in which judges easily could be bribed or intimidated by the Ku Klux Klan. These strategies of political repression were reinforced by the Supreme Court which, in 1883, declared the Civil Rights Act of 1875 unconstitutional. This act had secured the rights of all citizens to places of public amusement and to public accommodations and had stipulated that no person could be disqualified to sit on a jury because of his or her race. After the Civil Rights Act was struck down, it was no surprise when, in *Plessy v. Ferguson* (1896), the Court upheld a Louisiana law calling for separate railroad accommodations for blacks and whites. The Court ruled that laws were "powerless to eradicate racial instincts or to abolish distinctions based upon physical differences. . . ." This decision became the legal basis for Jim Crow laws in the South and for a segregated school system; this segregation met with resistance, but was not successfully challenged until the civil rights movement of the 1950s.

The regime of repression and violence in the South was based on economic relationships that reduced most blacks to living little better than they had under slavery. Most blacks did not own land. Although some had acquired land after the Civil War, many lost it when President Andrew Johnson restored confiscated land to white planters. Since most blacks did not have the money to buy their own land, they were either sharecroppers or sharetenants. The latter furnished their own stock and tools and received a portion of the crop they produced. The sharecroppers owned nothing except their labor. They needed credit for everything—tools, animal feed, fertilizer, cabins, etc. As a result, they were able to keep little of what they produced. Since landlords often doubled as merchants and were able to charge high prices for the things they sold, their tenants usually were heavily indebted to them and, therefore, incapable of improving their lot. After the crop failure of 1878, many blacks decided to emigrate to the Midwest, particularly to Kansas. However, in these areas of the country they also found racial prejudice and few employment opportunities.

The economic opportunities of black women during the post-Reconstruction period, in both the North and the South, were particularly limited. The largest percentage of black women worked on the land (38.4 percent), usually as sharecroppers, although some black women owned their farms. The rest were in domestic service (30.83 percent) or worked as laundresses (15.9 percent) and a small percentage worked in factories (2.76 percent).* Racial prejudice effectively barred most blacks from factory work in both the North and the South until the twentieth century. Although wages of black women were very low they were frequently the sole support of their families,

---

*Jean Collier Brown, "The Negro Woman Worker: 1860–1890," *Black Women in White America*, p. 252.

since their employment opportunities as maids or laundresses were more dependable than those available to black men. Relative to their numbers in the population, far more black than white women worked for wages. For example, in New York at the end of the nineteenth century, five percent of married white women worked for wages, while twenty-five percent of married black women worked for wages (these figures underestimate the paid work of both white and black women, since piece work done at home or the taking in of boarders— both common occupations for women—were not recorded in the census before 1910). The work of black women in supporting their families, in keeping them together, and in educating their children was often heroic. Ida B. Wells was not alone in this regard.

One of the major weapons used to keep black women in their place was what Gerda Lerner calls the myth of "the bad black woman."* A different level of sexuality was assumed for blacks and whites; accordingly, all black men were regarded as potential rapists and all black women as potential prostitutes. As one black woman wrote in 1902, "A colored woman, however respectable, is lower than the white prostitute."† As in the case of the slurs against Wells's character, whatever a black woman achieved, her character remained suspect. This myth was reinforced in the South in various ways: the denial of the title, "Miss" or "Mrs.," to black women;‡ taboos against mixing of the races; refusal to let a black woman customer try on her purchases in a store; the assigning of single toilet facilities to blacks but not to whites; the different legal sanctions for rape, sexual abuse of minors, or other sexual crimes committed against white and black women. The myth was used to justify the rape of black women during Reconstruction—acts that usually were committed to humiliate and terrorize women with politically active husbands. Since all black women were assumed to be loose by nature, rape could not exist.

Blacks responded to the political repression and to the acts of violence on many fronts. Immediately after the war, some, like Ida B. Wells and Sojourner Truth, attempted to use the courts to sue railroad companies that refused to seat blacks with whites; some, like

---

*Black Women in White America, pp. 164–172.
†Quoted in Black Women in White America, p. 166.
‡While these titles are regarded as sexist by many women today, in a period in which they were used universally for all white women, the refusal to address black women as "Miss" or "Mrs." was intended as a racist and sexist slur.

Frederick Douglass, Frances Ellen Watkins Harper, and Wells, appealed to the national conscience through their lectures and writing; others fought physically against the Jim Crow laws; some blacks fled the South to make homes for themselves in the North where, unfortunately, they found the same degree of racism as existed in the South but in different forms. Organizations were formed to protest segregation and lynching: the Afro-American National League in 1890, the National Association of Colored Women in 1895, and the National Association for the Advancement of Colored People in 1909.

All these forms of political protest would have been impossible without the existence of widely read black newspapers. In the late 1820s, newspapers in New York City attacked the relatively small free black community and its abolitionist activities. It was largely in response to these attacks that the first black newspaper, *Freedom's Journal*, was founded in 1827. Subsequently, more than twenty black newspapers were published in the antebellum period; these were addressed to ex-slaves and free blacks living in the North. They were instrumental in the development of political awareness among blacks in the North and in the development of the abolitionist movement. Mary Ann Shadd, the editor of the Canadian abolitionist newspaper, *The Provincial Freeman*, was the most prominent black woman journalist in the period before the Civil War.

After the Civil War, the black press continued to be essential to the cohesion, survival, and resistance of the black community. By 1900, there were approximately 150 weekly newspapers that were widely read among blacks. They provided news of the black community that could not be obtained in the regular press; they raised awareness in the black community about the extent and nature of racist oppression; and often urged resistance to discrimination among their readers. Although differing in political orientation, these newspapers usually took an uncompromising stand on issues of racial equality. They also provided their readers with examples of black women and men who achieved distinction in American life, thus fostering race pride which was essential in keeping the black community together and in maintaining its morale. Of course, as Dorothy Sterling indicates, these newspapers varied greatly in quality from the giants, such as the Indianapolis *Freeman*, the New York *Sun*, and the Chicago *Defender*, to small papers that mainly carried local news. But the latter newspapers had an important political function to play as well. Since blacks were entirely invisible in the white press, they had to turn to the black press for news of a marriage, a death, employment opportunities, a lost child, a church social, a lecture. Thus, the black press promoted cohesion in the black community, race pride, and resistance to racism not only through its political articles, but also through the reporting of the daily events of the black community.

Black women led the attack on lynching. Gerda Lerner states that "the work of black club women and later the NAACP on this issue is a direct outgrowth of Ida B. Wells's persistent muckraking journalism, exposés, lectures and organization."* At the beginning of the twentieth century, Mary Church Terrell also used hard hitting journalism as well as fine organizational skills to attack the lynching system. During these years, black women exhorted white women to speak out against lynching, since it was often done in their name. However, it was not until 1930 that white women joined together in the Association of Southern Women for the Prevention of Lynching— and then under considerable prodding from black women.

Ida B. Wells's attack on lynching was particularly bold and radical. Even to broach the taboo subject of sexual relationships between the races was revolutionary. Her arguments against lynching were based in part on evidence she collected to show that, in fact, in cases no rape had taken place. To document this, she had to take considerable personal risks, including interviewing the family, friends, and neighbors of the accused. In exposing the lynching system, she revealed the double standard of sexual morality in the South which called every relationship between a black man and a white woman rape, but which ignored and even sanctioned the rape of black women by white men.

In addition to leading the attack on lynching, middle-class black women formed clubs to improve conditions for themselves and their communities. Black women's societies had played an important part in the struggle for the abolition of slavery and in gaining equal rights for free blacks and women. After the Civil War, black women continued to form clubs that dealt with local educational and welfare issues. Most black women, like Wells, believed that their main concerns were the poverty of their communities, their own lack of opportunities, lynchings, and segregation. But some black women felt that it was also important to struggle for all women's rights and to

*Gerda Lerner, *Black Women in White America*, p. 198.

influence white women's organizations. Thus, women, like Wells and
Josephine St. Pierre Ruffin, who organized black women's clubs, attempted to be a part of white women's national organizations. Their
attempts were not always successful. Some, like Fannie Barrier Williams of Chicago, were rejected by the white women's clubs, and in
1900, Jacqueline St. Pierre Ruffin was told that she could not represent a "colored club" in the General Federation of Women's Clubs
(GFWC). Although this incident resulted in a debate on racism, the
GFWC maintained its segregationist policy for several more decades.

By 1894, when Ida B. Wells was conducting her crusade against
lynching, hundreds of black women's clubs existed all over the country. An attack on the character of black women, in a widely-publi-
cized statement by a leading Southerner, sparked these clubs to unite
into one organization. In response to Ida B. Wells's British lecture
tour against lynching, James Jack, president of the Missouri Press
Association, wrote to the British antilynching society that "the negroes in this country were wholly devoid of morality, the women
prostitutes and all were natural thieves and liars."* The outraged
response of black club women led to the formation of a new national
organization, the National Association of Colored Women (NACW),
in 1895.

Black club women's first order of business was to defend true moral
integrity as women and to redefine the criterion of "their womanhood." As Paula Giddings points out, the NACW challenged the Victorian ideas that restricted *all* women for it insisted that women
could and should struggle against the evils that undermined the society.

In order to achieve justice for the race as well as themselves the
club women excelled in organizing around local and regional issues
as well as national issues such as lynchings and segregation in travel
accommodations. Though its leadership was middle class, its membership was primarily working class, tenant farmers, and the poor.
This helped to keep the organization aware of the needs of ordinary
black women. Clubs such as the Phillis Wheatley Home Association
of Detroit and the Sojourner Truth Club of Montgomery, Alabama
helped organize country and city schools, libraries, colleges, homes
for the aged, day nurseries, and unions. Some clubs, like the Ida B.
Wells Club of Chicago, campaigned vigorously for the vote for
women. The NACW also helped to maintain and communicate the

---

*Quoted in *Black Women in White America*, p. 436.

culture of black people by promoting the study of black history in schools and by informing people about black artists.*

Leaders of the NACW included Josephine St. Pierre Ruffin, one of its founders and editor of the paper, *The Women's Era;* Margaret Murray Washington, president of the NACW from 1914–1918; and Mary Church Terrell, the organization's first president. By 1914, the NACW represented fifty thousand black women from all walks of life, in twenty-eight states, and more than one thousand clubs.

After 1914, the lives of black people changed considerably as a result of the great migration of blacks from South to North and the increasingly urban mold in which black issues began to be cast. This change, of course, affected black women. However, the gains made in the twentieth century have their roots in the struggle against lynching and segregation and the creation of educational and cultural institutions that newly freed black women of the nineteenth century helped to initiate.

The twentieth-century protest movement was dominated initially by the conflict of ideologies espoused by Booker T. Washington and W. E. B. DuBois. Booker T. Washington became extremely influential among blacks and whites in the late nineteenth century as a result of his willingness to accommodate segregation and disenfranchisement while encouraging blacks to concentrate on economic self-improvement. He did this primarily by founding a number of agricultural and technical black colleges, which educated an entire generation of black students, and through encouraging blacks to establish their own businesses and farms. Because of his accommodative views, he was lionized by white politicians and supported by business tycoons such as Andrew Carnegie. Carnegie gave money, for example, to Tusgekee Institute, which Washington founded. So great was his influence that presidents rarely made political appointments of blacks without consulting him. To some minds, his strategies helped to avert a disastrous race war. To others, his position resulted in the entrenchment of segregation and a loss of political rights that steadily eroded whatever economic gains blacks were making.

W. E. B. DuBois was a Harvard graduate and the first black to receive a Ph.D. in this country. Unlike Washington, he believed that blacks should receive the best education—not merely vocational or

*Among them Edmonia Lewis, the first American black to achieve recognition as a sculptor, and Phillis Wheatley, the eighteenth-century black poet.

technical—and that this educated elite, whom he called the most "talented tenth," would lead the struggle against discrimination and segregation. At a political conference in Niagara, in 1906, he outlined his philosophy of political protest: "We claim for ourselves every single right that belongs to a free-born American, political, civil and social; and until we get these rights we will never cease to protest and assail the ears of America." Although the Niagara Movement did not materialize into a mass-based political organization, several years later DuBois was instrumental in founding the National Association for the Advancement of Colored People (NAACP), which embodied the movement's militant philosophy. Wells was among the original fifty-three founders; throughout her life she espoused the more militant positions held by DuBois. Eventually, the NAACP was instrumental in making lynching a federal crime, in attacking school segregation, and in working on a broad front for political and civil rights as well as for social and economic justice.

Mary Church Terrell

In 1900, more than seven million of the eight and three-quarter million American blacks lived in the South. Between 1900 and 1910, 200,000 blacks left the South; and between 1910 and 1920, it is estimated that nearly a million trekked to the North. By 1920, the black population had doubled in the northeastern states and increased by sixty percent in the north central and western states. According to the census takers, at least as many black women as men took the journey north. Black men and women left the South for a variety of reasons, the most pressing of which were Jim Crow laws and poverty.

Black migration greatly increased after 1915 because of the boll weevil plague in the South and the availability of jobs in the North caused by World War I. Black newspapers such as the Chicago *Defender* encouraged blacks to leave the Jim Crow South. However, initial enthusiasm and hope soon gave way to dissatisfaction and despair as migrants were forced to live in impoverished and disease-ridden ghettoes. The demobilization of four and one-half million soldiers led to the firing and laying off of blacks; those who remained on the payrolls were crowded into the lowest-paying, menial jobs. The pattern of discrimination that blacks found in the North differed from that in the South. There were no "White Only" signs, no legal restrictions on voting, and no Jim Crow schools and public facilities; however, the color line was maintained just as effectively as in the South, primarily through discrimination in jobs and housing.

In 1919, race riots, unprecedented in their violence and numbers, occurred in more than twenty cities. The main cause was the competition between blacks and whites for jobs and housing following the war. The most extensive and violent of the riots took place in Chicago, resulting in 38 deaths and 537 injuries (see p. 112). Even president Woodrow Wilson, no friend of blacks, described the whites in these riots as the "aggressors."

By 1930, nine-tenths of all black women were still in farming or domestic service, as they had been since the Civil War; however, the majority now were employed as domestics. Domestic work was neither unionized nor subject to state regulation. Black women often earned much below the minimum wage, less than the amount required to keep one person from poverty, and they received no benefits from the New Deal social legislation, remaining without social security, worker's compensation, or unemployment insurance. By 1939, the median income of black women was only thirty-eight percent that of white women, and black women had the highest unemployment rate in the nation.*

In spite of the fact that black women were the most exploited workers, opportunitites did increase for them in the economic and cultural spheres. More black women were able to get jobs in manufacturing than previously, although clerical, sales, and government office jobs were not generally open to them until after World War II.† Because job opportunities for black men also increased, some black families were able to improve their standard of living. Some black women, like Madame C.J. Walker, a manufacturer of cosmetics, became wealthy entrepreneurs. And because of the growing popularity of jazz, fine black singers like Bessie Smith became nationally famous, making a significant impact on American music. In literature, novelists like Jessie Fauset, Nella Larsen, and Zora Neale Hurston were key figures in the Harlem Renaissance. In fact, not until the 1970s would black women publish as many novels.

In New York, the White Rose Working Home was created "to check the evil of unscrupulous employment agents who deceived the

---

*Today the median income of black women in ninety-two percent that of white women.
†The economic situation of black women began to improve somewhat after World War II as jobs in the service and clerical areas of the economy began to become available to them. It was not, however, until the 1960s that the economic situation of black women began to improve substantially through their increased employment in such fields as nursing, and social work, as well as sales and clerical work—areas traditionally dominated by white women.

unsuspecting girls desiring to come North." Started by Victoria Matthews, an ex-slave, the White Rose Working Home temporarily
housed the migrants, helped them find decent jobs, and taught them
domestic courses and black history. This home, like many others,
was absorbed into the New York League for the Protection of Colored
Women, which eventually became a national organization with
branches in major Northern cities. By the 1920s, the New York
League became a part of the Urban League which was deeply concerned with the problems of migrant black women.

Organized black women concentrated on two areas: 1) obtaining
education for black women, so that they could increase their chances
in the job market as well as participate more fully in all aspects of
American life, and 2) developing organizations for black workers—
men, women, and children. The following organizations all concentrated on these goals: the National Association for the Advancement
of Colored People (NAACP), the Urban League, the National Association of Colored Women (NACW), the "colored work section" of the
Young Women's Christian Association (YWCA), and the National
Council of Negro Women (NCNW). For a discussion of the NACW,
which was headed by Mary Church Terrell from 1896 to 1901, see
page xxxvi. The other major organization of black women, the
NCNW, was founded by Mary McLeod Bethune in 1931. It eventually
represented 850,000 black women, and it encompassed every kind of
club activity, which included supporting educational institutions,
working in the political arena for a federal antilynching law, and
developing self-help approaches for economic independence in poor
black communities. The NCNW is still very active; one of its primary goals in the 1970s was the alleviation of poverty in Sunflower,
Mississippi, one of the poorest counties in the United States.

It is impossible, in such a short space, to do justice to black wom-
en's achievements in creating and supporting educational institutions in the 1920s and 1930s. Mary McLeod Bethune was the leader
in this area, dedicating her life to the education of black women. In
1904, she started Bethune College for black women in a small shack
furnished with salvaged material from junkyards. In 1922, Bethune
College merged with Cookman College, the first college for the higher
education of black men in the state of Florida. As the college's guid-
ing light, Mary McLeod Bethune fundraised and impressed educational circles with the need to support education for black women.
Through the NCNW, she was able to make the education of blacks
during the Depression a matter of national concern. In 1936, she was
appointed by President Roosevelt to head the Division of Negro Af-

fairs of the National Youth Administration, thus becoming the first black person to hold such a high federal office. Her policies helped to improve the employment and educational possibilities for black youth amid the worsening conditions of the Depression.

Nannie Burroughs was another leader in education during this period. As secretary of the Women's Auxiliary of the National Colored Baptist Convention, she founded the National Training School for Girls in 1900. Its courses included homemaking, housekeeping, household administration, management for matrons and directors of school dining rooms and dormitories, interior decorating, laundering, and home nursing. Aware that black women usually were relegated to domestic work, Nannie Borroughs sought to give this work respectability. She also organized the National Association of Wage Earners in 1931 to aid migrant black women in securing a wage that would allow them to live decently.

Just as Nannie Burrough's work in education led her to develop the National Association for Wage Earners, black women workers and educators saw that education was not sufficient to improve their opportunities. Education did not guarantee employment, and employment did not guarantee a living wage or preclude discrimination on the job. Consequently, black women began to organize unions in those industries that employed black women in significant numbers—laundries, cleaners, dyers, and garment industries—and in many instances they were on the first committees that helped to formulate union policies. Some of these women were Charlotte Almond, Phoebe Symond, Roberta Randolph, Sabina Martinez, and Ida J. Dudley. One of the major unions affected by black women was the Tobacco Workers Union in Winston-Salem, North Carolina. Especially important was the organizing work of Moranda Smith, one of the leaders in the union and the first woman to serve as a regional director for an international union in the South. The Sharecroppers Union and the Tenant's League also owed their existence to black women. In 1934, Dora Jones established the Domestic Workers Union in New York which focused on perfecting a contract to protect the domestic worker on the job. Though her attempts were short-lived because of the difficulties inherent in organizing domestic workers, some of the ideas and tactics that she developed are being used today in more successful union drives among domestic workers.

Black women were active in the suffrage movement in spite of the discrimination they experienced. Ida B. Wells, Josephine St. Pierre Ruffin, Mary Church Terrell, and Mary McLeod Bethune were among the most prominent black suffragists. The National American Women's Suffrage Association (NAWSA) was intent on winning Southern states to their suffrage cause, and the only way they could get the support of Southern women or members of Congress was not to challenge white supremacy in the South. Thus, in 1899, the NAWSA officially declared that black suffrage and women suffrage were separate issues—even though historically the two issues always had been linked. In 1903, the organization supported a states' rights policy, meaning that every state could determine the qualifications of the members in its suffrage organizations and could, if it chose, accept white supremacy doctrines. Although officially the NAWSA did not endorse racist policies, and its oldest members remained deeply opposed to them, by separating the two issues of black and women suffrage, it gave tacit support to the assumption that in the South women suffrage meant white women suffrage. Many suffragists, in fact, agreed with NAWSA president Carrie Chapman Catt who saw in women suffrage a way of outvoting immigrants in northern cities and of maintaining white supremacy in the South.* In spite of these overtly racist views and policies, black women gave the suffrage movement their support, recognizing the importance of the vote for black women in the North. They organized black women, participated in parades, and stood outside the White House in vigils. Some white women were strong enough to oppose racist policies: a group of white women from Illinois linked arms with Ida B. Wells in the 1913 Washington suffrage parade, after she had been asked officially not to march with the Illinois delegation.

During World War I, black women met humiliating discrimination when they tried to offer their services to the government. Mary Church Terrell reports that not only were all government offices segregated, but preference in these divisions was given to light-skinned blacks. After the Nineteenth Amendment was won, black women such as Mary Church Terrell were active in Republican Party politics. Their tasks were assigned on a segregated basis: they were in charge of organizing black women to vote. The first black women to be appointed to federal government positions were Mary McLeod Bethune and Crystal Bird Fauset—both appointed by Franklin Delano Roosevelt. While some black women were elected to state and local offices, the main political activities of black women occurred outside electoral politics—in their work for federal legislation on lynching,

*Carrie Chapman Catt was NAWSA president from 1900 to 1902 and from 1915 to 1919.

in their efforts to fight Jim Crow laws through legislation and in the courts, in their struggles for decent schools for blacks, and in their community organizing. Black women were usually the key grassroots organizers; they also held leadership positions in civil rights organizations. Here was where their real strength lay, and their contributions in this period laid the ground for their work in the civil rights movement of the 1950s and 1960s.

Barbara Christian

Black History:
A Selected Table

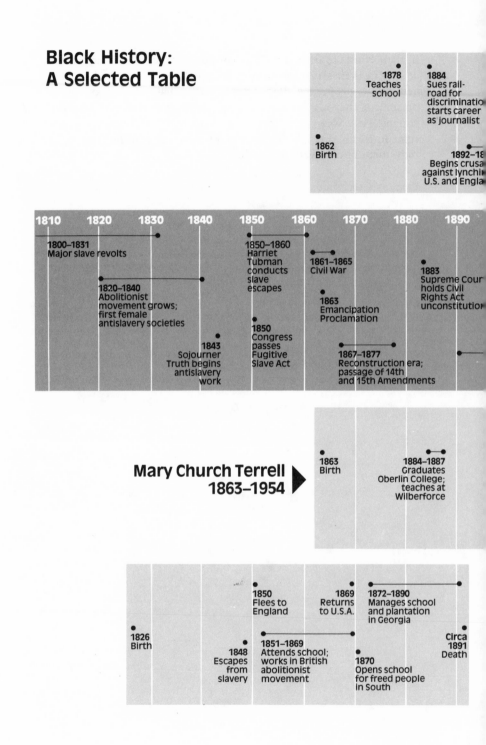

1878
Teaches
school

1884
Sues rail-
road for
discrimination
starts career
as journalist

1862
Birth

1892–18
Begins crusa
against lynchi
U.S. and Engla

1810	1820	1830	1840	1850	1860	1870	1880	1890

1800–1831
Major slave revolts

1820–1840
Abolitionist
movement grows;
first female
antislavery societies

1843
Sojourner
Truth begins
antislavery
work

1850–1860
Harriet
Tubman
conducts
slave
escapes

1850
Congress
passes
Fugitive
Slave Act

1861–1865
Civil War

1863
Emancipation
Proclamation

1867–1877
Reconstruction era;
passage of 14th
and 15th Amendments

1883
Supreme Cour
holds Civil
Rights Act
unconstitution

Mary Church Terrell
1863–1954 ▶

1863
Birth

1884–1887
Graduates
Oberlin College;
teaches at
Wilberforce

1826
Birth

1848
Escapes
from
slavery

1850
Flees to
England

1851–1869
Attends school;
works in British
abolitionist
movement

1869
Returns
to U.S.A.

1870
Opens school
for freed people
in South

1872–1890
Manages school
and plantation
in Georgia

Circa
1891
Death

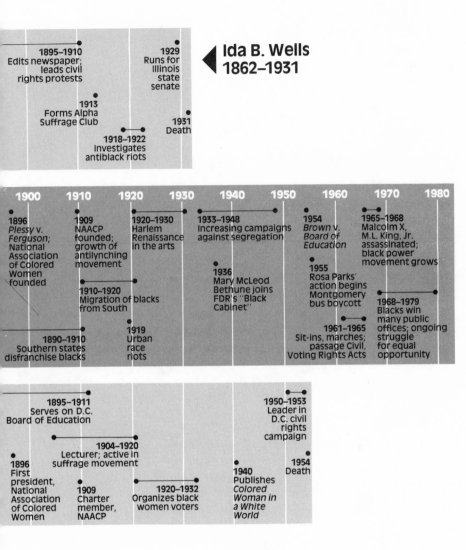

1895–1910
Edits newspaper;
leads civil
rights protests

1929
Runs for
Illinois
state
senate

◀ **Ida B. Wells**
1862–1931

1913
Forms Alpha
Suffrage Club

1931
Death

1918–1922
Investigates
antiblack riots

1900	1910	1920	1930	1940	1950	1960	1970	1980

1896
Plessy v.
Ferguson;
National
Association
of Colored
Women
founded

1909
NAACP
founded;
growth of
antilynching
movement

1920–1930
Harlem
Renaissance
in the arts

1933–1948
Increasing campaigns
against segregation

1954
Brown v.
Board of
Education

1965–1968
Malcolm X,
M.L. King, Jr.
assassinated;
black power
movement grows

1936
Mary McLeod
Bethune joins
FDR's "Black
Cabinet"

1955
Rosa Parks'
action begins
Montgomery
bus boycott

1910–1920
Migration of blacks
from South

1968–1979
Blacks win
many public
offices; ongoing
struggle
for equal
opportunity

1890–1910
Southern states
disfranchise blacks

1919
Urban
race
riots

1961–1965
Sit-ins, marches;
passage Civil,
Voting Rights Acts

1895–1911
Serves on D.C.
Board of Education

1950–1953
Leader in
D.C. civil
rights
campaign

1904–1920
Lecturer; active in
suffrage movement

1896
First
president,
National
Association
of Colored
Women

1954
Death

1940
Publishes
*Colored
Woman in
a White
World*

1909
Charter
member,
NAACP

1920–1932
Organizes black
women voters

◀ **Ellen Craft**
1826–1891

Black
Foremothers

Three Lives

For Emily and Daniel,
whose generation can carry forward
the promise of these lives.

ONE:
Ellen Craft

The Valiant Journey

FOUR MILLION AFRO-AMERICAN WOMEN were slaves in the years between 1619 and 1865. Of that vast throng, the history books mention only a handful, reporting on their lives with scant detail. What of those faceless, nameless millions who plowed the fields, cooked the meals, nursed the white folks' babies during the long, dark years? What did they feel and think? What were their aspirations? How did they view the world around them?

The answers to these questions are hard to come by. Slave women kept no diaries, rarely wrote letters. Even their names were not listed in the census records. Yet here and there, over the centuries, individuals spoke out briefly, took some action, left a mark on the history of their time.

One of these slaves was Ellen Craft, who for a few short years was the best-known black woman in the United States. Overshadowed by her husband during her lifetime, she has been overlooked by historians. But her story, pieced together

Chronology

1826: Ellen born, Clinton, Georgia, to Maria Smith, slave, and her master, Major James Smith.

1837–46: To Macon, Georgia, as slave in household of Major Smith's daughter, Eliza, and her husband, Robert Collins. Meets William Craft, young slave and carpenter; they are allowed to "marry."

1848–50: Ellen and William Craft make daring escape to freedom, eventually settle and work in Boston.

November 7, 1850: Ellen and William Craft legally married by the Rev. Theodore Parker. Fugitive Slave Law forces them to flee to England.

1850–69: Crafts work in abolition movement, attend Ockham School and teach there. They have five children: Charles, b. 1852; William, b. ca. 1855; Brougham, b. ca. 1857; Ellen, b. 1861; Alfred, b. ca. 1869.

1870: Returning to the United States, the Crafts lease a southern plantation. Ku Klux Klan burns it.

1872–78: Crafts buy Woodville, a plantation near Savannah. Ellen Craft starts school for neighboring children; teaches newly-freed women rudiments of housekeeping; manages plantation, while her husband travels in the North to raise money for the school.

1878: Ellen Craft goes to Boston to testify in libel suit brought by her husband. Meets her nephew, James A. Healy, Catholic bishop of Portland, whom she has not seen since childhood in Clinton.

1878–ca. 1890: Ellen and William Craft continue to live and work at Woodville plantation.

1890–ca. 1891: Crafts move to Charleston, South Carolina, to live with daughter, Ellen, a leader in the women's club movement, and her husband, William Crum, physician and political activist.

Ca. 1891: At Ellen Craft's death she is buried, at her request, under a pine tree at Woodville.

from the accounts of her contemporaries, shows a woman of
superb courage, intelligence, and integrity who gave impetus
to the antislavery movement before the Civil War and leadership to the newly freed people afterward.

Born a Slave

Ellen was born in Clinton, Georgia, in 1826, just fifty years
after the Declaration of Independence had said that "all men
are created equal." Her father was Major James Smith, a lawyer
and surveyor; her mother, Maria, was one of Smith's slaves.

Clinton was still frontier country when Major Smith and
his wife, Eliza, settled there in 1810. His military title may
have been acquired in the Creek War of 1812–14, which ended
with the cession of two-thirds of the Creeks' territory to the
United States. At war's end he helped to survey the newly
acquired land and to lay out county and town lines. By the
time of Ellen's birth, he was one of the richest men in central
Georgia, the owner of a hotel and plantation in Clinton, land
in Macon and other parts of the state, and about a hundred
slaves.

One of his contemporaries described Major Smith as a
typical planter who

took his "drams" when he felt like it, used profane language except
in the company of women, paid his debts, voted his party ticket and
worked many Negroes, to whom he was kind in his own imperious
way. . . . He was over six feet, large framed, ruddy-faced, with a voice
like a bassoon when he let it out. In his roomy mansion he dispensed
a hearty hospitality to neighbors, lawyers and friends, sold his crops
and occasionally a Negro, thought himself a good citizen and felt sure
he was sound on politics and fox-hunting.

No description exists of Ellen's mother, Maria. All that is
known of her is that she was of light complexion, implying
that she too had had a white father. Born around 1808, she
was purchased by the Major when still a child and was trained
to be what her society called a "house wench." She did her
share of cooking, scrubbing, and the thousand-and-one other
tasks that made up "woman's work" then, but most of her
time was probably spent as nurse to the Smith children. There

was a new Smith baby every second year; the oldest was only three years younger than Maria.

As a house servant, Maria had some advantages over her sisters who toiled in the fields. While they were scantily clad and fed, she ate the leftovers from her master's table and wore her mistress's cast-off clothes. She also acquired the speech and manners of white Georgians. Her superior status was of little help, however, when Major Smith took to visiting her cabin at night. She was seventeen then, with no way to defend herself against this man who owned her as absolutely as he owned his horses and hunting dogs. Rape of a slave woman? There was no law forbidding it in Georgia's statute books.

Maria's daughter was born in the same year in which the Major's wife gave birth to a fifth son, Elliott. The resemblance between the two children and their father must have been striking, so much so that Ellen's childhood was scarred by it. Little Ellen's worst times came when there were visitors. Clinton, the county seat of Jones County, was only fifteen miles from Milledgeville, the state capital. When court was in session in Clinton or the legislature was meeting in Milledgeville, lawyers and politicians from other parts of the state stopped at the Smith plantation. As the gentlemen had their drinks on the verandah, one of them was sure to comment politely on the youngsters playing nearby.

"What beautiful children, ma'am," a guest might say. "I'd a known that little girl was the Major's daughter if I'd a met her in Savannah. She looks so much like him."

Then Mrs. Smith, her face flushed and her voice tight, would order Ellen to go around to the cookhouse to find Maria. After the visitors left, the child could expect boxed ears or a slap that left her face tingling.

A devout Methodist and a dutiful wife who bore her husband's children uncomplainingly, Eliza Smith was consumed with anger at his relations with slave women. Her situation was a familiar one in the South. "We are complimented with the names of wives, but we are only the mistresses of harems," one planter's wife complained. Another wrote, "Like the

patriarchs of old, our men live all in one house with their
wives and concubines and the mulattoes one sees in every
family resemble the white children. My disgust sometimes is
boiling over." However, instead of venting their anger at their
husbands or at the institution of slavery, they tended to blame
those who were doubly victimized, their female slaves. Thus
Mrs. Smith took revenge on little Ellen.

Nor could Ellen look to her father for sympathy. Some
masters were genuinely fond of their "yard children" and
made provisions to free them, but the Major did not fall into
this category. When Ellen was three, he sold another of his
slave daughters, Mary Eliza, to Michael Healy, a neighboring
planter. Healy, an Irishman who had come to Georgia after
the War of 1812, flouted southern law and tradition by treating
her as his wife and taking their children to the North to be
educated. Ellen undoubtedly knew the Healys and could contrast their home life with her own. She would meet her Healy
nephews many years later, under vastly different circumstances.

Meanwhile, if Major Smith had any paternal feelings toward
Ellen, she was not aware of them. In later years she spoke of
him only as her master. His wife she recalled as "incessantly
cruel."

No matter how much love Maria gave her daughter, she
was unable to protect her from Mrs. Smith's tongue-lashings
and blows. A weaker child might have been crushed, but
Ellen, with a sturdiness that was to serve her well throughout
life, managed to close her ears to the harsh words, to duck the
blows or bear them stoically. At last when she was eleven, a
change in the Smith household brought relief from her mistress's persecution.

The Smiths' eighteen-year-old daughter, Eliza, was engaged
to be married to Dr. Robert Collins of Macon, a wealthy
widower almost old enough to be her father. On the eve of
the wedding Mrs. Smith announced that she was giving Ellen
to Eliza as a wedding present, to serve as her personal maid.

Ellen must have heard the news with a mixture of anger
and dismay. Could the Smiths really give her away as if she

were no more than a silver tea service or a damask table-cloth? She soon found out that they could. Eliza and Robert Collins were married on April 27, 1837. A day later when they drove off in their carriage, Ellen accompanied them to Macon.

Situated on land taken from the Creek Indians, the fourteen-year-old town of Macon had begun as a handful of log cabins on the banks of the Ocmulgee River. But as flatboats and paddle-wheeled steamers began to transport cotton and lumber from the back country, it quickly became a bustling young metropolis. By the time of Ellen's arrival, the busy streets along the waterfront were lined with banks and hotels, law-yers' and newspaper offices, and the population had grown to four thousand, almost equally divided between black and white, slave and free.

Ellen's new master—a husband acquired his wife's property at the time of their marriage—was one of the town's most prominent men. A leader in all manner of civic enterprises, he contributed to the support of a militia company that fought for Texan independence, and he helped bring the railroad and telegraph to Macon. The home that he had built for his bride was in a new section of town, on a hill overlooking the river and the surrounding countryside. Set in four acres of pine forest, it was described as "an elegant mansion" with broad verandahs and white columns flanking the doorway. As a lady's maid, Ellen probably helped her mistress to dress in the morning and carried her reticule when she went to market or to pay calls. At night when there were guests, she would have been on duty to tie corset laces, button shoes and bodice, and assist with the cluster of false curls that every fashionable woman wore to frame her face. Afterwards, there would be the undressing ritual when curls were combed out, and dress and petticoat put away just so. A lady's maid usually slept on a pallet outside her mistress's bedroom in order to be in earshot if her mistress woke during the night and needed her.

It was a long day for an eleven-year-old, but there was one saving grace. Eliza Collins had not inherited her mother's cruel temper. She demanded efficiency from her servant-sister, but she seldom scolded and never struck her. Although Ellen later said that Eliza was more humane than most slaveowners, no bond of affection tied the half-sisters together. Slavery laid down certain ground rules. A slave had to know and keep her place. She had to be made to feel inferior. Some slaveowners accomplished this with whips, others with words.

"Did they call you 'nigger'?" a northern woman asked Ellen many years afterwards. "Oh yes," was the reply. "They didn't call me anything else. They said it would make me proud."

Macon was twelve miles from Clinton—a considerable distance in those preautomobile, pretelephone days—and Ellen, who had never before been separated from her mother, must have been lonely. But in 1838 Major Smith moved his family to Macon, to a house on First Street along the river, and Ellen and Maria were reunited. On Sundays, when they were allowed time together, they wandered through the town and the neighboring woods.

Just up the hill from the Collinses' mansion was the campus of Georgia Female College (now Wesleyan College). Built by the same contractor who had put up the Collinses' house, it was the grandest building in town, a four-story brick edifice that housed classrooms, dormitories, library, and chapel. In 1840 it became the first college in the world to confer degrees on women.*

Ellen must have seen the college often, both with her mother and with her mistress, whose husband was one of the school's incorporators. She could not, of course, dream of studying there. A Georgia law made teaching slaves to read or write a crime. Although an occasional kind mistress flouted the law, Eliza Collins was never moved to do this. Thus Ellen, living across the road from the first college for women, remained illiterate.

Her mistress did, however, encourage one of Ellen's talents—sewing. Ready-made clothing and sewing machines were still in the future, so that Ellen's skill with a needle

---

*Coeducational Oberlin College admitted women from the time of its founding in 1833; but not until 1844 was a woman granted its standard degree.

was an important asset, particularly after the Collinses' first baby was born. By the 1840s Ellen was spending most of her time as a seamstress. She was permitted to move to a one-room cabin of her own, in the woods behind the big house, where she could keep bolts of cloth and sewing implements. There she had some measure of privacy.

As the years passed, and Ellen grew in strength and grace, she began to make friends outside of the Collinses' household. Slaves did much of the work, both simple and skilled, in Macon. The women were cooks, nurses, dressmakers, hair-dressers, washerwomen, working in hotels and shops as well as in private homes, while the men were barbers and butchers, blacksmiths and bricklayers, carpenters, coachmen, and so on. Many masters hired out their slaves on a yearly basis; others permitted them to hire their own time. This meant making their own contracts with employers and boarding and clothing themselves. They paid their owners a fixed sum each year; any money earned above their expenses was their own.

These hiring practices gave the Macon slaves more mobility than their country cousins. Although they still had to show passes if they went out after curfew, they could stop at a grog shop on their way home from work, visit with friends, meet slaves from other parts of town. On Sundays and during the week between Christmas and New Year's, there were parties and dances and a chance for an unsupervised exchange of news and gossip.

Perhaps it was at one of these parties that Ellen first met William Craft, an apprentice in a cabinetmaker's shop. As a child, William had seen almost his entire family—mother, father, brothers, sister—sold, one by one, to planters in differ-ent parts of the state. Around 1841, when his owner, a mer-chant named Craft, needed money again, he mortgaged Wil-liam and his one remaining sister, Sarah, to a Macon bank. After speculating in cotton futures, Craft was unable to meet the mortgage payments, and William, aged sixteen, and Sarah, fourteen, were sold at public auction.

Sarah was sold first, knocked down to a planter who lived some distance away. Standing on the auction block, William watched her drive off in her new master's cart. The frightened child gave him a last appealing glance, tears trickling down her cheeks, then buried her face in her lap. It was a searing experience for William, one that he never forgot.

Ira H. Taylor, a cashier at the bank, purchased William and sent him back to the cabinetmaker's shop. After his apprenticeship was completed, he was permitted to hire his own time—a privilege for which he paid Taylor $220 a year. Working days as a cabinetmaker, he waited on tables at night at the hotel across the street, in exchange for board.

Although the friendship between Ellen and William soon ripened into love, Ellen refused to consider marriage. She had seen so many slave families torn apart that she was afraid of a commitment that could be set aside by their masters at any time. Besides, marriage meant children—children who would belong to Robert Collins and not to her and William. With the destruction of his own family a vivid memory, William could do little to reassure her. It was then that they began to talk about running away.

Despite their inability to read, they knew that there was a place "up North" where black people were free, and that there were "damned abolitionists" there who wanted to end slavery. But "up North" was a thousand miles from Macon. Even if they could get past the patrollers who guarded the roads at night, even if they could fool the bloodhounds trained to catch runaways, there were still mountains and rivers and dark, impenetrable swamps to cross. Fugitives like Frederick Douglass and others whose activities were reported in the Macon newspapers had escaped from the border states, never from the deep South.

A generation earlier, black Georgians had run away to Florida to live with the Seminoles or had made their way to Mexico. These escape routes were no longer open. The Seminole strongholds had fallen; the Indians and their black allies had been shipped across the Mississippi to Indian Territory. Now United States troops were invading Mexico in a war that slaveowners hoped would extend slavery south of the Rio Grande.

Perhaps it was the beginning of the Mexican war that convinced Ellen that escape was impossible and that she might as well try to find a measure of happiness in slavery. Some time around 1846, she and William asked their owners' permission to marry. Slave marriages were simple affairs, without legal or religious formality. After all, there was little logic in promising to be faithful "till death do us part" when either partner could be sold away. As soon as Collins and Taylor gave their permission, William moved into Ellen's cabin, and together they worked to make it a home. While Ellen sewed, William built furniture, including a fine chest of drawers fitted with a lock, where their savings were kept. When they closed their cabin door at night, they could temporarily forget the world outside.

Their happiness was clouded by the fear of having a child who could be sold or mistreated. Modern birth control was unknown, but there were crude homemade devices—sponges, hollowed-out halves of citrus fruits, even stones—that some desperate slave women used to prevent conception. Whether or not Ellen tried any of these, they could have done little to allay her anxiety. After two years of living together, they once again began to talk about running away.

The scheme that they evolved was a daring one. Ellen, who could easily pass as white, would disguise herself as a planter's son, an invalid gentleman traveling north to consult doctors, while William went along as her servant. They had savings sufficient to pay their fares as far as Philadelphia.

Ellen shrank from the idea at first, afraid of failure. To run away and then be caught could mean jail, whipping—possibly sale to a house of prostitution, where light-skinned slave women brought premium prices. But when she considered the hopelessness of their present situation, she agreed to try. Once the decision was made, they worked quickly. Christmas was eight days away and discipline was lax during the holiday season. If they could get passes to visit friends in the country, they might be able to reach the North before their absence was noticed.

While Ellen made herself a pair of trousers, William went from store to store buying the rest of her outfit. As he told the story a dozen years later, most of the details that made her disguise plausible were devised by Ellen. Realizing with a sudden pang that she would be asked to sign hotel registers, she made up a bandage and sling for her right arm to explain her inability to write. A poultice—a bulky wet bandage—tied from chin to head, toothache-style, would conceal her beardlessness. Then, looking in a mirror, she saw that her eyes might register fear, anger, dismay, and she sent William downtown for a final purchase—a pair of green spectacles.

On the eve of their departure, William cut her hair off square at the back of her neck, in the style of a Dutch bob, and helped her dress. With a tall beaver hat to complete her costume, she made "a most respectable-looking gentleman," he said. One wonders how she felt as she paced the cabin, practicing a man's stride. Did she enjoy the freedom that the trousers gave her—or did she feel embarrassed in that time, three years before the famous bloomer costume was introduced? William later said that Ellen "had no ambition whatever to assume this disguise and would not have done so" if there had been another way to freedom.

Just before dawn on December 21, 1848, they left the cabin. When William locked the door for the last time, the enormity of the undertaking overcame Ellen. Recovering from the moment of panic and grief that seized her, she squeezed William's hand. They parted to take separate routes down the hill to the railroad station. Hers took her near the Smiths', where Maria still lived. She must have paused, wondering if she would ever see her mother again. But the first rule for runaway slaves was "no good-byes," and she walked on.

Flight to the North

No motion picture could fully convey the drama of the next days. From the moment that Ellen walked up to the stationmaster and asked for tickets to Savannah for "William Johnson and slave" she was, so to speak, on camera. William was in the background playing the part of faithful servant, but the brunt of the impersonation fell on her.

Tickets in hand, they seated themselves quickly, William up front in the Jim Crow car and Ellen in a first-class carriage.

As the train pulled away from the station, she found, to her dismay, that the man sitting next to her was Mr. Cray, a friend of Dr. Collins who had known her since her childhood. He had dined with the Collins family only the day before. Were they on her trail already?

"A fine morning, sir," Cray remarked.

Pretending to be deaf, Ellen kept her face toward the window. Cray repeated the remark in a louder tone. As she continued to ignore him, a passenger behind them laughed.

Annoyed, Cray raised his voice. "I'll make him hear," he said. "It's a fine morning, Sir."

Afraid to keep silent any longer, Ellen replied with a toneless "Yes," then turned again to the window. Finally he gave up and began to talk with the other travelers—on "the three great topics of discussion in first-class circles in Georgia, namely Niggers, Cotton, and the Abolitionists," William later reported. When Cray left the car at the next station, Ellen breathed a little easier. One hurdle had been passed—but there would be others.

The train rumbled along, hour after hour, through forests of tall Georgia pine, past red clay hills and fields of cotton and corn. By late afternoon the hills had given way to marshland, the pines were scrub, and the slaves in the fields were burning the stubble of last fall's rice crop. But Ellen—although she had never ridden on a train before—could not have paid much attention to these changing scenes.

At Savannah, an omnibus carried them across town to the wharves. The stars were shining in the December sky when they walked up the gangplank of the steamer *General Clinch*, bound for Charleston, South Carolina. A steamer was more intimate than a train. Passengers ordinarily gathered in the saloon to eat and talk together, then slept in common gentlemen's and ladies' cabins. Pleading illness, Ellen retired immediately to the gentlemen's cabin, leaving William to prepare fresh poultices to make her absence plausible.

The following morning she could no longer postpone meeting her fellow passengers. At breakfast, where she was seated next to the captain, she found that everyone was curious about her. Eating with her right hand in a sling was awkward, the conversation even more so. But while William solicitously cut up her food, she managed to answer questions about her health and travel plans. The success of her masquerade was attested to by a shipboard companion who gave his impressions of the Crafts a fortnight later, after their identity was known:

I had gone early on board, and having got tired of reading the papers, amused myself with watching the passengers. My attention was attracted by the appearance of a young man who entered the cabin supported by his servant, a strapping Negro. The man was bundled up in a capacious overcoat. His face was bandaged with a white handkerchief and its expression entirely hid by a pair of enormous spectacles. He appeared anxious to avoid notice and before the steamer had fairly left the wharf requested, in a low womanly voice, to be shown to his berth, as he was an invalid and must retire early—his name he gave as Mr. Johnson. His servant was called and he was put quietly to bed.

I awoke in the morning with the sun shining in my face. It was a mild, beautiful morning, and most of the passengers were on deck, enjoying the freshness of the air and stimulating their appetites for breakfast. Mr. Johnson soon made his appearance, arrayed as on the night before, and took his seat quietly upon the guard of the boat. He was a slight built, apparently handsome young man, with black hair and eyes, and of a darkness of complexion that betokened Spanish extraction. Any notice from others seemed painful to him so to satisfy my curiosity, I questioned his servant, who was standing near, and gained the following information.

His master was an invalid—he had suffered for a long time under a complication of diseases that had baffled the skill of the best physicians in Georgia—he was now suffering principally with the rheumatism and was scarcely able to walk. He came from Atlanta, Georgia and was on his way to Philadelphia, at which place resided his uncle, a celebrated physician, and through whose means he hoped to be restored to perfect health.

This information, communicated in a bold, offhand manner, enlisted my sympathies for the sufferer although it occurred to me that he walked rather too gingerly for a person afflicted with so many ailments.

The boat docked at Charleston at mid-morning. While the other passengers disembarked, Ellen and William hung back,

fearful that their absence had been discovered and that their
masters had telegraphed to have them arrested. When no one
stepped forward to claim them, Ellen hobbled across the wharf
with William's help and directed a carriage driver to take
them to the best hotel in the city.

"Poor Mr. Johnson," the invalid gentleman, was shown to
a room—and for the first time in thirty hours, Ellen was able
to remove parts of her disguise. But not for long. William
returned to tell her that the steamer they had planned to
take to Philadelphia did not run during the winter months.
However, they could travel by boat to Wilmington, North
Carolina, and complete their journey by train. A steamer was
leaving that afternoon. There was barely time for a meal
before their departure.

Bandages and glasses in place, jacket brushed and boots
well polished, Ellen entered the hotel dining room. At tables
nearby, some of the wealthiest and most influential gentlemen
of the South were enjoying their noonday meal. While William
ate in the kitchen, three slave waiters danced attendance on
the young invalid. She made sure to tip them generously when
she left.

At the Customs House office on the wharf, they ran into
trouble. Charleston, the leading slave port on the Atlantic
coast, had strict regulations governing the movements of
black people. Anyone taking a slave from the state had to
convince the customs officer of her right to do so. When
Ellen asked for tickets to Philadelphia for "Mr. Johnson and
slave," the officer eyed her suspiciously.

"Boy, do you belong to that gentleman?" he asked William.

William's prompt "Yes, sir" appeared to satisfy him. Hand-
ing Ellen the tickets, he pushed the Customs House book
toward her, saying, "Register your name here, sir, and the
name of your nigger, and pay a dollar duty on him."

The dreaded moment had come. Ellen coolly paid the dollar;
then, pointing to her bandaged hand, she asked the officer to
sign for her. His suspicions aroused again, the officer refused.

The room was crowded with people waiting to buy tickets.
Before Ellen had a chance to reply, a passenger from the
General Clinch with whom she had breakfasted that morning

stepped out of line to greet her. His affability heightened by the brandy he had been drinking, he assured one and all that he vouched for "Mr. Johnson—know his kin like a book."

The atmosphere in the Customs House changed abruptly. While Ellen fought off her "friend's" invitation to a drink and cigar, the captain of the North Carolina vessel came forward. "I'll register the gentleman's name and take the responsibility," he said; and "William Johnson and slave" were soon aboard the vessel, heading north.

During the trip, the captain stopped Ellen to explain, "It was not out of disrespect to you, but they make it a rule to be very strict at Charleston. If they were not careful, any damned abolitionist might take off a lot of valuable niggers."

After disembarking at Wilmington the following morning, the Crafts took a train to Richmond, Virginia. From Richmond, they had another wearying night and day of travel. A train to a small station beyond Fredericksburg, a steamer up the Potomac to Washington, then another train to Baltimore.

The train chugged along at thirty miles an hour, a dizzying speed in those days, but never fast enough for Ellen. Tired, hungry, covered with soot from the wood-burning locomotive up ahead, she had only one thought in her mind. Their passes expired on the day after Christmas. Would they reach the free states before their absence was discovered?

William walked back from the Jim Crow car as often as he dared, to see how his "master" was faring, but for much of the time she was on her own. During the ride to Richmond, a father and two marriageable daughters overwhelmed the "poor young gentleman" with sympathy. The young ladies insisted that she lie down, using their shawls for a pillow, while the father gave her a recipe for a cure for rheumatism and an invitation to visit them on her next trip to Virginia. Thanking him for his kindness, Ellen was careful to put the recipe in her waistcoat pocket quickly. There was always a chance that she would hold it upside down if she pretended to read it.

Not all of the interchanges were pleasant. One woman insisted that William was her slave who had run off the year before. A man warned Ellen that she was spoiling William

by saying "thank you" when he did her a service; another
filled her with tales of "ungrateful niggers." Ellen, growing
more anxious with each passing hour, avoided the conversations as best she could.

On Christmas Eve they reached Baltimore, the last stop
before the free states. After helping Ellen to board the Philadelphia train, William went off to find his own accommodations. He had one foot on the steps of the car when a conductor
tapped his shoulder.

"Where are you going, boy?" he asked.

"To Philadelphia, sir," William replied. "I'm traveling with
my master who's in the next carriage."

"You'd better get him out and be mighty quick about it,
because the train will soon be starting. It's against my rules
to let any man take a slave past here unless he can satisfy
them in the office that he has a right to him."

As Ellen hurried to the railroad office with William, she
realized that their lives depended on what she did and said
in the next moments. Squaring her shoulders under her man's
cloak, she faced the stationmaster.

"Do you wish to see me, sir?"

"Yes," he said. "It's against the rules to carry a slave out
of Baltimore without proof of ownership. We can't let any
slave pass here without receiving security to satisfy us that
it is all right."

Ellen, who had lived among upper-class southerners all her
life, knew how they talked to underlings. In her best imperious
manner she insisted, "I bought tickets in Charleston to pass
us through to Philadelphia. You have no right to detain us."

Could they have come so close to freedom, only to be
driven back? No jovial friend stepped forward as in Charleston,
but the onlookers in the office were clearly on "Mr. Johnson's"
side. Why, just to hear him speak, anyone would know he
was a gentleman, and very ill, besides.

Ellen was pondering her next step when a bell rang, announcing the train's departure. She stared at the stationmaster,
as if challenging him, and he dropped his eyes.

"I really don't know what to do," he muttered. "I calculate
it's all right." While she held her breath, he told a clerk to

tell the conductor to "let this gentleman and slave pass. As he is not well, it's a pity to stop him here."

Thanking him brusquely, as if she had received nothing but her due, Ellen took William's arm and limped across the platform. As she settled in her seat, the train departed with a great puff of steam. In nine hours they would be in Philadelphia.

Ellen sat up through the long night. At Havre de Grace, passengers were asked to leave the cars while they were shunted onto a ferry that crossed the Susquehanna River. For the first time, William was not on hand to assist her; he had fallen asleep in the baggage car and had been moved onto the boat with the luggage, without awakening. She had some bad moments wondering what had happened to him. But he was jolted awake as the train got under way again and came back to reassure her.

One A.M. Two A.M. Three A.M. Had they crossed the Pennsylvania border? In the darkness, there was no way to tell. An hour before dawn, she could see flickering lights in the distance. Another passenger nudged his companion to say, "Wake up, we're at Philadelphia!"

The train pulled into the station soon afterwards, and William bundled her into a cab. A companion in the Jim Crow car had given him the name of a boardinghouse kept by abolitionists. As the horses trotted down the cobbled streets, their hooves breaking the Sunday silence, Ellen burst into tears.

It was Christmas morning and they were free.

Free at Last

The next days were a blur to Ellen. She had moments of exhilaration, when, once more in women's clothing, she tossed the bits and pieces of her disguise around the room. Then reaction set in, and the sleepless nights and anxious days took their toll. Exhausted physically and emotionally, she rested in her room at the boardinghouse, while news of the Crafts' escape spread to antislavery circles in the city.

Before long, the boardinghouse parlor was crowded with visitors: men like Robert Purvis, "president" of the Underground Railroad, and William Still, chairman of the Philadelphia Vigilance Committee, who was in charge of forwarding fugitives to Canada. Although they had helped hundreds of runaway slaves, they had never heard a story quite like the Crafts'. Ellen must have changed into her disguise for their benefit, for decades later, when he compiled a history of the Underground Railroad, Still wrote:

Never can the writer forget the impression made by their arrival. Even now, after a lapse of nearly a quarter of a century, it is easy to picture them in a private room surrounded by a few friends—Ellen in her fine suit of black, with her cloak and high-heeled boots, looking, in every respect, like a young gentleman. In an hour after having dropped her male attire, and assumed the habiliments of her sex, the feminine only was visible in every line and feature.

Their new friends advised them not to remain in Philadelphia, which was too close to the slave states to be safe, but to push on to Boston. Ellen, however, who was, according to Still, "physically very much prostrated," needed rest before she made another move. Arrangements were made to send them to the home of Barclay Ivins, a Quaker farmer who lived in Penn's Manor, some twenty-five miles outside the city.

Ellen was under the impression that Ivins, like Purvis and Still, was a light-skinned black man. She didn't discover her mistake until she and William arrived at his home, and his wife and daughters came out to greet them.

She stood stock-still in the yard, refusing to enter the house. "William," she whispered, "I thought we were coming among colored people."

William, who had learned from Purvis that the Ivinses were trustworthy, tried to reassure her. "It's all right," he said. "These are the same."

"No, it's not all right," she insisted, "and I'm not going to stop here. I have no confidence in white people. They are only trying to get us back to slavery. I'm going right off."

She was heading for the road when Mrs. Ivins took her by the hand and said, "How art thou, my dear? Come in to the fire. I dare say thou art cold and hungry after thy journey."

Ellen allowed herself to be led indoors but made it clear with every line of her rigid body that she was not going to stay.

"Take off thy things and sit near the fire," Ivins urged. "Supper will soon be ready."

"Come, Ellen, let me assist thee." As Mrs. Ivins began to untie her bonnet strings, Ellen backed away. The habits of a lifetime were hard to discard. In her twenty-two years, no white woman had ever put out a hand in friendship before.

Motherly Mrs. Ivins understood her misgivings. "I don't wonder at thee being timid, but thou needs not fear us. We'd as soon send one of our daughters into slavery, as thee. Make thyself at ease."

Still wary, Ellen agreed to take off her outer clothing. The conversation went on around her, until, gradually, the family's kindliness broke down her defenses. As William later reported, "Her fears and prejudices vanished and from that day she has believed that there are good and bad persons of every shade of complexion."

When the supper dishes were cleared from the table, the Ivinses' daughters brought out spelling books and slates and offered to teach their guests to read and write. Ellen and William exchanged embarrassed glances, afraid that they were too old to learn. They had managed to teach themselves the alphabet in Macon, but anything beyond that seemed hopeless. But the young women were so eager to share their knowledge that the Crafts awkwardly set to work. By the end of their stay in Penn Manor, they were able to write their names quite legibly and had made some progress in reading and spelling.

They had been at the Ivinses' farm for more than a week when they had their first visitor, William Wells Brown. A slave who had escaped fifteen years earlier, Brown was a lecturer for the Massachusetts Anti-Slavery Society. Self-educated, he had already published a best-selling autobiography and a collection of antislavery songs; over the next years, as novelist, playwright, and historian, he would become America's first black man of letters. Learning of the Crafts' escape while lecturing in Philadelphia, and realizing the impact they would have on northern audiences, he had come to ask them to accompany him to a series of antislavery meetings in New England.

For Ellen and William, freedom—the dream that they had cherished for so long—meant a chance to work, to have a home and family. Knowing nothing about the abolitionist movement, they had not anticipated a role in it. But they could see that Brown, who came from a background similar to their own, knew his way around the new world he was describing to them. Reassured by his self-confidence, they were readily persuaded to accept his invitation.

Parting from the Ivins family was hard. Their daughters had given Ellen the affection that she had never had from her own half-sister, and she felt as if she were leaving members of her family. For more than thirty years, she continued to correspond with them.

Before leaving Pennsylvania, Brown wrote to William Lloyd Garrison, editor of *The Liberator*. His letter, the first published account of the Crafts' escape, appeared in *The Liberator*'s January 12, 1849, issue:

Here is a wonderful case—read it!
SINGULAR ESCAPE.
Pineville, (Pa.) Jan. 4, 1849

Dear Friend Garrison:

One of the most interesting cases of the escape of fugitives from American slavery that have ever come before the American people, has just occurred, under the following circumstances:—William and Ellen Craft, man and wife, lived with different masters in the State of Georgia. Ellen is so near white, that she can pass without suspicion for a white woman. Her husband is much darker. He is a mechanic, and by working nights and Sundays, he laid up money enough to bring himself and his wife out of slavery. Their plan was without precedent; and though novel, was the means of getting them their freedom. Ellen dressed in man's clothing, and passed as the *master*, while her husband passed as the *servant*. In this way they travelled from Georgia to Philadelphia. They are now out of the reach of the blood-hounds of the South. On their journey, they put up at the best hotels where they stopped. Neither of them can read or write. And Ellen, knowing that she would be called upon to write her name at the hotels, &c., tied her right hand up as though it was lame, which proved of some service to her, as she was called upon several times at hotels to "register" her name. In Charleston, S. C., they put up at the hotel which Gov. M'Duffie and John C. Calhoun generally make their home, yet these distinguished advocates of the "peculiar institution" say that the slaves cannot take care of themselves. They arrived in Philadelphia, in four days from the time they started. Their history, especially that of their escape, is replete with interest. They will be at the meeting of the Massachusetts Anti-Slavery Society, in Boston, in the latter part of this month, where I know the history of their escape will be listened to with great interest. They are very intelligent. They are young, Ellen 22, and Wm. 24 years of age. Ellen is truly a heroine.

Yours, truly,
WM. W. BROWN.

P. S. They are now hid away within 25 miles of Philadelphia, where they will remain until the 6th, when they will leave with me for New England. Will you please say in the Liberator that I will lecture, in connexion with them, as follows:—

At Norwich, Ct., Thursday evening, Jan. 18.
" Worcester, Mass., Friday evening, 19.
" Pawtucket, [R.I.] Saturday evening, 20.
" New Bedford, [Mass.] Sunday afternoon and evening, 28.

With the publication of Brown's letter, Ellen and William were launched on the antislavery circuit. At the annual meeting of the Massachusetts Anti-Slavery Society held at Faneuil Hall, Boston's famed "cradle of liberty," they were greeted with cheers and thunderous applause. Wendell Phillips, the movement's most eloquent speaker, called their escape "an incident of courage and noble daring" and predicted that "future historians and poets would tell this story as one of the most thrilling tales in the nation's annals and millions would read it with admiration."

In spite of their devotion to the antislavery cause, most white abolitionists were not free from a belief in white superiority, even in the matter of personal appearance. Samuel May, general agent of the Anti-Slavery Society, revealed this when he described the Crafts in a letter to an English friend:

Ellen Craft, the young wife, is a woman who may well be called beautiful. She has no trace of African blood discernible in her features —eyes, cheeks, nose or hair, but the whole is that of a Southern-born

white woman. To think of such a woman being held as a piece of
property, subject to be traded off to the highest bidder (while it is in
reality no worse or wickeder than when done to the blackest woman
that ever was) does yet stir a community brought up in prejudice
against color a thousand times more deeply than could be effected
in different circumstances. . . . William Craft, the husband, is a dark
mulatto, tall, erect and dignified in his appearance, of good mind,
good judgment, and every way giving proof of a manly self-reliance
and self-respect.

A woman observer was somewhat less enthusiastic about
Ellen's appearance, finding her "a pretty nice looking girl
with straight black hair. . . . Her behavior was pretty and
natural."

For the next four months, the Crafts crisscrossed Massachusetts: Springfield . . . Brookfield . . . Northborough . . . Marl-
borough . . . New Bedford . . . Lowell . . . Salem. . . . Traveling
by stagecoach and train, boarding at antislavery homes, they
made public appearances in more than sixty towns.

An astute showman, Brown planned each meeting with
care. Before their arrival in a new place, placards announced
that "William W. Brown accompanied by the Georgia fugitives
will speak at Town Hall tonight." "The Georgia fugitives"
were a welcome diversion in the long New England winter,
and halls were filled to overflowing before the appointed hour.
Brown opened each meeting with introductory remarks, then
asked the Crafts to step forward. After William Craft told
the story of their escape—"in a very modest and becoming
manner," according to The Liberator—Brown gave an anti-
slavery speech of more general interest, then brought "the
fugitive couple" to the front of the platform again "so that
all present might have the pleasure of seeing them." The
meeting ended with antislavery songs sung by Brown and a
collection for the benefit of the Crafts and the Anti-Slavery
Society.

Although the two Williams did all the talking, it was Ellen
who aroused the greatest interest. Most northerners had never
seen a woman slave before. Harriet Tubman was still in
Maryland, her escape some months away, and Sojourner

Truth's powerful voice was just beginning to be heard in western Massachusetts. "An expression of astonishment arose" when Ellen appeared at a meeting in New Bedford, its chairman reported. "Surely many of the mothers, wives, and sisters in the audience must have felt the question of slavery brought close home to their hearts as they looked upon her."

Women were not encouraged to speak in public, but after William addressed a meeting in Northborough, there were murmurs in the audience: "I want to hear his wife." At first Ellen replied to a few questions; by mid-April she had become a regular part of the program. "Mrs. Craft gave a very particular account of their escape," *The Liberator* said. "It was told in so simple and artless a manner as must have carried conviction to the mind of everyone present."

Beginning with their first public appearance, the Crafts had a difficult decision to make. Should they tell their full story, giving the city they had come from and the names of their masters? Most fugitives—including Brown and Frederick Douglass—suppressed these details and took new names when they reached the North, for fear of being apprehended. The fear was a real one. The Constitution required authorities in the free states to surrender runaways to their masters; a Fugitive Slave Law passed in 1793 put teeth in the original article. But the Crafts' story was so unusual that their friends urged them to tell it as circumstantially as possible in order to convince skeptics that it was true. More than once, members of their audiences questioned them closely about details of their life in Georgia. Had they refused to answer, they might have been considered impostors.

Ellen had another reason for agreeing to a full disclosure. It was her only way to let her mother know that they were safe. A letter to Maria Smith would be intercepted, but newspaper stories about "the Georgia fugitives" would be noted by the southern press. Sure enough, the February 13, 1849, issue of Macon's *Georgia Telegraph* reprinted a New England newspaper article about the Crafts. The *Telegraph* editor added a note at the end: "The Mr. and Mrs. Crafts who figure so largely in the above paragraph will be recognized at once by

our city readers as the slaves belonging to Dr. Collins and
Mr. Ira H. Taylor, of this place, who runaway or were decoyed
from their owners in December last."

Ellen could be confident that Maria would know their
whereabouts—and so would Collins and Taylor. The Crafts'
decision to avoid anonymity was to affect the entire course
of their lives.

After months of traveling with Brown, Ellen and William
grew restive. The first heady weeks, when the bare fact of
freedom was a day-to-day marvel, were over. Now they wanted
to settle down and start their new life. For Ellen, who had no
desire to become a public figure, the constant display must
have been distasteful. Wherever she went people crowded
around to shake the hand of "the white slave."

Several times the couple tried to return to Boston, only to
be urged to continue because they were "doing the cause a
good service." At one meeting, after William said that he
planned to work at his trade again, a member of the audience
offered a resolution:

That it is the opinion of this convention that the labors of Mr. and
Mrs. Craft, accompanied by those of an antislavery agent, would do
much to hasten the deliverance of the captive, as well as prove highly
beneficial to the cause of freedom generally.

When the resolution passed unanimously and was backed
up with a collection taken for their benefit, the Crafts felt
obliged to continue. "The cause," after all, was close to their
hearts, too. In May, however, when Brown left for a meeting
in New York, to be followed by a European trip, they were
free to begin their private lives once more.

Boston, they soon discovered, was a divided city. In anti-
slavery Boston, black people were invited to speak at public
meetings, serve on committees, and join with whites in all
aspects of the struggle. Proslavery Boston confined black
children to one lone segregated school, denied blacks pews in
churches and admission to places of public entertainment.
And then there was black Boston, a community of freeborn
blacks and fugitive slaves. Living, for the most part, on the
narrow streets behind the State House in a section known as

"Nigger Hill," they had their own churches, clubs, and meeting halls.

Antislavery Boston welcomed the Crafts with a meeting at Tremont Temple at which William Lloyd Garrison and Wendell Phillips spoke, but it was in black Boston that they found a home. Their first friends there were Lewis and Harriet Hayden, a fugitive slave couple who had arrived in the city some years earlier and who kept a boardinghouse and Underground Railroad station at Number 66 Phillips Street.* A decade older than William and Ellen, Lewis Hayden was a respected member of both antislavery and black Boston, moving freely between the two worlds.

After arranging to board with the Haydens, the Crafts set about finding work. Despite William's training as a cabinetmaker, no one would hire him. Blacks were barred from all of the skilled trades, not only by employers, but by journeymen and apprentices who refused to work alongside "niggers." After some discouraging weeks, he opened a secondhand furniture store on Federal Street.

His job-hunting experiences were not unique. In 1849 black Boston could boast of two lawyers and one dentist; the other men were servants, common laborers, or small tradesmen. Curiously enough, white abolitionists showed little awareness of the employment problems that their black associates faced. In speeches then, and in later reminiscences, the white men who were closest to the Crafts said that William worked as a cabinetmaker in Boston. None seemed to know that he had been barred from his trade.

Ellen encountered none of William's difficulties. Her storied courage, her middle-class speech and manners, so different from the black stereotype held by most whites, made her easily acceptable among them. She was an immediate favorite of the antislavery women. These women were the backbone of the movement. While their husbands were the public speakers, they did the day-to-day work of fund raising and pamphlet writing. Oppressed themselves—their first meetings broken up by jeering men who told them to go back to the kitchen—they

* The Hayden home still stands, a stop on Boston's Black Heritage Trail.

were more sensitive to the needs of individuals. Even before William's store was established, Ellen was working as a seamstress in homes on Beacon Hill and Tremont Street. In some, at least, she found genuine sympathy and friendship.

Later, when she decided to learn upholstering so that she could recover the worn couches and chairs that William bought and sold, one of her new friends introduced her to an upholsterer, a Miss Dean. On days when she didn't have a sewing job to go to, she worked with Miss Dean, learning the new trade.

The months sped by quickly. Only occasionally did Ellen remember that they were still fugitives, in danger of recapture. Once Isaac Scott, a white man from Macon who owned one of William's brothers, visited the furniture store. He had come, he said, to give William a chance to buy his brother's freedom. Afraid that Scott's real errand was to recapture Ellen and himself, William closed the store immediately, and for a few days he and Ellen went into hiding. But when Scott failed to pursue them, the store was reopened in a new location on Cambridge Street. Their savings mounted, and they were beginning to talk about a home of their own, when the Congress of the United States destroyed their newfound feeling of security.

In the continuing struggle for power between North and South, congressmen from the two regions had negotiated a compromise: California was admitted to the Union as a free state, and the slave trade (but not slavery) was abolished in the District of Columbia. In return for these concessions, the South was rewarded with a new harsh Fugitive Slave Law. If a white man took an oath that a black was his runaway slave, federal marshals and United States Commissioners were obliged to return him or her to slavery, while "all good citizens" were "commanded to aid and assist them." Blacks were denied the right to testify in their own behalf or to have a jury trial; whites who aided them could be fined $1,000 and imprisoned for six months.

The new law meant that any black—fugitive or freeborn— could be seized and taken to the South on the word of any white. President Millard Fillmore signed the law on September

18, 1850. His signature was scarcely dry when panic-stricken black people from all over the North packed their belongings and fled to Canada. Forty men and women left Boston that month, and a hundred refugees from Pennsylvania and the border states arrived to take their places.

Night and day, knots of anxious blacks gathered in the Haydens' parlor. Should they join the exodus or stay to fight the law? At a "Meeting of Fugitives" at the African Meeting House on October 4, black Boston voted to organize a League of Freedom, "to resist the law, rescue and protect the slave at every hazard." Lewis Hayden was elected president at the meeting, William Craft a vice-president.

Antislavery Boston backed up the fugitives with a huge rally at Faneuil Hall ten days later. Charles Francis Adams, son and grandson of presidents, chaired the meeting; Wendell Phillips and Frederick Douglass gave the main addresses. Black people, Douglass said, had vowed to die rather than return to slavery. Gesturing toward Ellen and William Craft, who had seats of honor on the platform, he asked the audience if it would permit a fugitive to be captured in Boston. Looking down upon the sea of faces, Ellen heard their shouted "No, no, no!"

Before the meeting adjourned, a Committee of Safety and Vigilance was organized "to secure the colored inhabitants of Boston from any invasion of their rights." The Reverend Theodore Parker, the city's most popular minister, was chairman of the committee. Its members included well-known white citizens—lawyers like Wendell Phillips, Richard Henry Dana, and Ellis Gray Loring, who was a United States Commissioner; the physicians Henry Ingersoll Bowditch and Samuel Howe—and such black leaders as Robert Morris, also a lawyer, Lewis Hayden, and William C. Nell. "I am happy to state," Frederick Douglass wrote the next day," that the public meeting held here has done much toward quieting the colored people."

Outwardly calm, Ellen followed her familiar routine. Trudging up Phillips Street to work each morning, she must have wondered when the blow would fall. What would a slave catcher look like? Would Dr. Collins himself come to Boston, bringing Eliza with him? She didn't have to wait long to find out.

A week after the Faneuil Hall meeting, a young man from Macon called at William's store. He was John Knight, who had worked with William in the cabinetmaker's shop. Oozing cordiality, Knight explained that he had come north to buy machinery for a new factory but hadn't wanted to pass up the chance of seeing his old friend. Wouldn't Bill take the afternoon off to show him the sights of Boston?

Begging off because he had work to finish, William guardedly asked, "Did you come alone?"

"Yes," Knight said, "There's nobody with me." After chatting pleasantly for a few minutes longer, he left. The next day he was back to invite William and Ellen to visit him at the United States Hotel, where he was staying. As an inducement, he offered to give Ellen news of her mother and to carry a letter back to Maria. Later that day a messenger brought a badly spelled note, reinforcing the invitation:

Oct 22 1850

Wm Craft—Sir—I have to leave so Eirley in the morning that I cold not call, so if you want me to carry a letter home with me, you must bring it to the united States Hotel to morrow and leave it in Box 44 or come your self to morro Eavening after tea and bring it. let me no if you come your self by sending a note to Box 44 U.S. Hotel so that I may no whether to wate after tea or not by the Bearer. If your wif wants to se me you cold bring her with you if you come your self

JOHN KNIGHT

PS I shall leave for home eirley a Thursday morning. J.K.

Questioning the messenger, who was a porter from the hotel, William learned that Knight had a companion, a short sandy-haired fellow named Hughes. Hughes! Every slave in Macon knew Willis Hughes, the town jailer. There was no longer any doubt about Knight's mission. Boston had its first case under the new Fugitive Slave Law.

When William and Ellen failed to respond to Knight's invitation, the slave hunters tried to find a judge or United States Commissioner who would issue a warrant for the Crafts' arrest. It wasn't easy. Two of the commissioners—Ellis G. Loring and George S. Hilliard—were antislavery men. Others were sympathetic or preferred not to get involved in what could only be an unpleasant business. But Hughes kept up a relentless pressure, and at last, on October 25, a judge issued the warrant.

Ellen was working with Miss Dean at a clergyman's home on Mt. Vernon Street when Mrs. Hilliard dropped by. One of Ellen's good friends, she had been delegated to take her to a safe hiding place. "I proposed to Ellen to come and do some work for me, intending not to alarm her," she recalled. "My manner which I supposed to be calm, betrayed me and she threw herself into my arms, sobbing and weeping. She, however, recovered her composure as soon as we reached the street and was *very firm* ever after."

Assured that William was safe, barricaded in his store, she agreed to go with Mrs. Hilliard. That afternoon Dr. Bowditch drove her to the neighboring town of Brookline, where Ellis Loring had a home. He and his wife were away, but their niece, Mary Carson, welcomed her. Despite Mary Carson's kindness, Ellen spent a wakeful night. When she slept, it was to dream that slave hunters were chasing her, while Daniel Webster, the Massachusetts statesman who had supported the Fugitive Slave Law, pointed a pistol at her head.*

The next day was endless. "She helped me make a new dress," Mary Carson wrote. "I watched her with admiration, she showed such great self control, such perfect sweetness of temper and grace of manner. She could hear nothing from her husband all day and of course might suppose him in every danger but she kept back her tears and kept up her sweet looks, till late in the afternoon a messenger came with news of her husband and messages directly from him."

The news, as far as it went, was good. The excitement in the city was so intense that the marshal's office had not yet served the warrant for their arrest. Black and antislavery Boston were working in unison to obstruct the slave catchers.

---

*Ellen related her dream the next day to Mary Carson. Carson's account of the incident is given in "William and Ellen Craft," *The Freedmen's Book*, by Lydia Maria Child (Boston, 1865).

While black men and women lined Cambridge Street to guard William's store, vigilance committee lawyers had Hughes and Knight arrested, charging that they had slandered William Craft by saying that he had stolen himself and his clothes when he left Georgia. The pair were out on bail, but the committee was plotting further ways to harass them.

On Sunday, when the marshal's office was closed, Dr. Bowditch insisted that William spend a quiet Sabbath with Ellen. Privately he thought that it might be the last day they would ever have together. Like most abolitionists, the doctor had always believed in nonviolence. On this occasion, however, he drove to Brookline with his buggy reins in one hand and a pistol in the other, while William carried both pistol and revolver. Fortunately there was no need to use the weapons, but Dr. Bowditch kept his in a place of honor in his library for the rest of his life.

When it was rumored on Monday that the Crafts were in Brookline, the Reverend Theodore Parker, armed with a hatchet, drove out to fetch them. He brought Ellen to his home, while William set up a command post at the Haydens'. In addition to an arsenal of guns and dirks, William and Hayden rolled a keg of gunpowder into the basement, prepared to blow up the house if the marshal's men broke in.

Theodore and Lydia Parker lived on Exeter Place, a narrow dead-end street on the opposite side of the Common from "Nigger Hill," in the heart of antislavery Boston. Wendell Phillips's home was around the corner, and the Garrisons were within a five-minute walk. Ordinarily Ellen would have enjoyed the comfortable clutter of the Parker home, where books covered every wall, overflowing onto the stairs and even into the bathing-room. Forbidden the first floors for fear that casual visitors might see her, she spent most of her daytime hours in Parker's fourth-floor study, which housed the finest private library in the city. While Lydia Parker mothered her young guest, her husband wrote his Sunday sermon, he said, "with a sword in an open drawer under my inkstand, and a pistol in the flap of the desk, loaded and ready."

None of this was mock heroics. Ellen and William had vowed to resist the slave hunters, even if it meant sacrificing their lives. In a conversation with Frederick Douglass that was reported in the newspapers, William refused to run away, saying, "Our people have been pursued long enough. If I can't live here and be free, I will die!"

"I don't wish to advise you," Douglass had replied, "but if you die our people will live!"

Respecting their courage, their friends made ready to defend the Crafts by any means necessary. Placards posted throughout the city warned of "SLAVE HUNTERS IN BOSTON." Following an unflattering description of the two men, Hughes was quoted as saying, "I am the Jailer at Macon. I catch negroes sometimes. I am here for Wm and Ellen Craft and damn'em I will have them if I stay till eternity, and if there are not men enough in Masschusetts to take them I will bring them from the South. It is not the niggers I care for—it is the principle of the thing." The placard ended, "MEN OF BOSTON!! SHALL THESE VILLAINS REMAIN HERE?"

Wherever Hughes and Knight went, they were pursued by crowds shouting "bloodhounds," "slave hunters," and threatening to pull them from their carriage. The vigilance committee lawyers had them arrested again and again: for slandering Ellen, for damaging William's business, for smoking and swearing in the streets, for carrying concealed weapons, for driving too fast. But after each arrest, some proslavery man came forward with bail, and they were back on the streets again. The lawyers even planned to have Ellen and William arrested so that as prisoners of Massachusetts they could not be taken from the state. This plan must have given the pair some bad moments, for the lawyers' proposed charge was fornication—because Ellen and William were not legally married.

Before this became necessary, Hughes and Knight, caving in after two weeks of psychological warfare, took the train to New York. Their departure did not mean safety for Ellen and William, however. As newspapers, North and South, described the incident, their freedom became a national issue. While Macon's *Georgia Telegraph* published an extra to deplore "the indignation, abuse and injustice" heaped on Hughes, Robert

(*text continued on page 36*)

A JOURNEY

Far right: Ellen Craft, in a photograph taken after escape to England. **1,2:** Drawing of Craft in disguise, with story in *London Illustrated News,* April 19, 1851. **3:** Lithograph of a railroad notice requiring identification of black passengers, 1858. **4:** A slave family in Georgia, ca. 1860. **5:** American Anti-Slavery Society publication, 1840. **6:** Engravings of Ellen and William Craft in middle age, from William Still's *The Underground Railroad,* 1872. **7:** Poster warning against slave catchers, April 24, 1851. **8:** Great Exhibition, Crystal Palace, London, 1851; antislavery demonstrations took place here.

1

—VOL. I. NO. 5.—

THE
AMERICAN
ANTI-SLAVERY
ALMANAC,
FOR
1840,

BEING BISSEXTILE OR LEAP-YEAR, AND THE 64TH OF AMERICAN INDEPENDENCE. CALCULATED FOR NEW YORK; ADAPTED TO THE NORTHERN AND MIDDLE STATES.

Slave State — *Free State*

NORTHERN HOSPITALITY—NEW YORK NINE MONTHS' LAW.
The slave steps out of the slave-state, and his chains fall. A free state, with another chain, stands ready to re-enslave him.

Thus saith the Lord, Deliver him that is spoiled out of the hands of the oppressor.

NEW YORK:
5 PUBLISHED BY THE AMERICAN ANTI-SLAVERY SOCIETY, NO. 143 NASSAU STREET.

PHILADELPHIA, WILMINGTON
AND
BALTIMORE RAILROAD.

NOTICE TO
COLORED PEOPLE

All Colored People (Bond or Free) wishing to travel on the Philadelphia, Wilmington and Baltimore Railroad, will be required to bring with them to the TICKET OFFICE, President Street Depot, some

RESPONSIBLE WHITE PERSON,

A Citizen of Baltimore, known to the undersigned, to sign a bond to the Company before they can proceed.

PASSENGERS FROM THE SOUTH OR WEST

Having Colored Servants, will please prepare themselves to comply with the above rule before proceeding to the Depot, as it will save them much trouble and vexation.

WM. CRAWFORD, Agent.
BALTIMORE, March, 1858.

3

6

FUGITIVES FROM SLAVERY.—REMARKABLE

RETURN IN THE CENSUS.

re reminded by Mr. Russell's powerful denunciation of Slavery of a re-
able instance of its baneful effects, which has just been illustrated by means
census return in Yorkshire. It appears that William and Ellen Craft have
been relating, at the Woodhouse Mechanics' Institute, a touching account o
escape from slavery ; and as they sojourned with Mr. Wilson Armistead, of
, on the 30th of March, it was requisite that their names and places of
ry, as well as their rank and profession, should be inserted by him in the
nment Census paper to be filled up and returned on the 31st. These
individuals were accordingly entered by Mr. Armistead under their
a-ignation "*Fugitives from Slavery in America, the land of their nativity !*"
s a startling entry, perhaps more extraordinary than any in the new return
population.

particulars of the escape of these fugitives from slavery are of the most
tic character. William and Ellen Craft were reared in Georgia, under
nt masters ; but, living near to each other they became eventually man and
William is a black man, but his wife Ellen is nearly white. Whenever
net, after their marriage, they contrived and discussed plans of escape ;
1848 this was accomplished : the wife, with her hair cut off, and wearing
spectacles, disguised herself as a young man, and her husband as her
r servant. They first travelled to Savannah, and then took the steamboat
arleston, in Carolina. After escaping many dangers of betrayal, and
g now expended their savings in obtaining their liberty, they settled in
s, William to work at his trade of cabinet-making, and Ellen to work with
eedle. In this way they maintained themselves, learned to read and
at evening schools, until the Fugitive Slave-law came into operation, and
very first evening they attended the school the warrant was issued for
apprehen-ion, and the slave-catchers were abroad in Boston. The excite-
and agitation of the three or four days' hunt in Boston were extreme ; but
m and Ellen ultimately succeeded in getting on board a British vessel,
the kidnappers were at New York.

fugitives arrived about four months since in Liverpool, where, for the
me, they set foot on really free soil. They are very interesting and intel-
persons. Ellen is twenty-four years of age, and as fair as most of her
sisters. William is very dark, but of a reflective, intelligent countenance.

ELLEN CRAFT

4

8

Collins wrote to President Fillmore asking him to enforce the law of the United States.

Fillmore's reply—aimed at placating the South—advised Collins that he had not yet exhausted all his legal remedies in the attempt to capture the Crafts. If all judicial proceedings failed, however, it would then be the president's "duty to call forth the militia, and use the army and navy."

When newspapers reported that the president was sending six hundred soldiers to Boston, Ellen and William agreed to leave the country. On the advice of George Thompson, a British abolitionist who was visiting in Boston, they decided to go to England. With the word "fornication" still ringing unpleasantly in their ears, there was one piece of business to take care of before their departure.

On the night of November 6, William C. Nell hurried across the Common to Exeter Place. Would Theodore Parker marry Ellen and William Craft? The following morning, Parker went to the Haydens', where bride and groom were waiting. On entering the room, he noticed a Bible lying on one table and a bowie knife on another. After the ceremony, he gave William the Bible and charged him to use it to save his own and his wife's soul. Then he took up the knife.

"I put that in his right hand, and told him if the worst came to the worst to use that to save his wife's liberty or her life," Parker wrote. "I told him that I hated violence, that I reverenced the sacredness of human life, and thought there was seldom a case in which it was justifiable to take it; that if he could save his wife's liberty in no other way, then this would be one of the cases."

There was no time for toasts to the bride and groom. Although a British steamship company had been operating between Boston and Liverpool for a decade, the Crafts did not dare to board a vessel in Boston Harbor. The vigilance committee had arranged to send them to Halifax, Nova Scotia, where the steamers stopped to refuel before crossing the Atlantic. The Reverend Samuel May accompanied them as far as Portland, Maine, leaving them at the home of Mr. and Mrs. Oliver Dennett, Underground Railroad stationmasters.

From there they were to travel by coastwise steamer to Nova Scotia.

In the dead of winter, it was a difficult trip at best, and this time almost everything possible went wrong. The Portland steamer rammed into another boat and had to put up for repairs. There was a further delay in New Brunswick. Then the stagecoach that was carrying them overland to Halifax overturned, and they walked the last seven miles of the trip in a downpour of rain. Bruised, cold, muddy, they reached Halifax only to find that their steamship had sailed two hours earlier, and they would have to wait a fortnight for the next one.

Once they crossed the Canadian border, they were safe from slave hunters, but prejudice dogged them everywhere. In New Brunswick and in Nova Scotia, Ellen had to pose as white in order to engage a hotel room. The innkeeper in Halifax was so unpleasant when she found that she had "nigger boarders" that, after a day, the Crafts moved out to stay with a black family.

Unwell when she left Boston, Ellen caught a fresh cold after the stagecoach mishap and was verging on pneumonia when the S.S. *Cambria* arrived in late November. The vigilance committee had given the Crafts one hundred fifty dollars, only enough for steerage accommodations, so that Ellen spent the crossing in a dark, crowded cabin in the hold of the ship, seasick and feverish, while William paced the deck, wondering if she would survive. Not until the passengers crowded to the rail for their first glimpse of the British coast did Ellen manage to dress and join them.

A day later, the *Cambria* docked in Liverpool. It was mid-December 1850, and their two-year odyssey was over.

English Years

Unsure of themselves in this strange new land, the Crafts stayed at a hotel in Liverpool for a few days, then gratefully accepted an invitation from a local minister and his family. They had letters of introduction to other antislavery people, but before they could present them, word came from an old friend. William Wells Brown had been in England for more than a year, lecturing and writing. He was scheduled to tour Scotland and wanted the Crafts to accompany him. Ellen, still shaky from her illness, remained with the minister's family while William joined Brown. Early in January, she traveled to Edinburgh to meet them.

Once more they were on the road, traveling from city to city to appear at antislavery meetings. But this trip was different from the New England tour in many ways. The British antislavery movement, which had won liberty for the slaves of the West Indies and was now supporting the American freedom struggle, was made up of "the best people": titled ladies and gentlemen, members of Parliament, ministers, doctors, literary folk. Prince Albert, Queen Victoria's husband, was president of the Anti-Slavery Society, giving it the seal of respectability that the American movement lacked. Instead of putting up at New England farmhouses, the three ex-slaves stayed in big city hotels or fine country homes. Their meetings were held in large halls where thousands came to see them.

Still a showman, Brown exhibited a panorama, a large backdrop showing scenes from the lives of American slaves that a London artist had painted for him. With a nice blend of drama and pathos, he told the stories of the slaves depicted in the panorama, sang songs, and sold copies of his books. It was good propaganda—and good entertainment, as well. William followed with a matter-of-fact report of their escape from Georgia. The Victorian code forbade women speaking in public, but Ellen, who was seated on the platform, was usually asked to "present herself to the audience." "She seemed rather reluctant to do so," a Scottish newspaper reported, "but on the persuasion of several gentlemen, she consented to occupy a standing position. She was most enthusiastically received. At first she seemed abashed, but the cheering having continued, she courtesied gracefully and retired. She is an intelligent and delicate good-looking woman."

Outside of meetings, Ellen was the focus of attention. Black women were a novelty in Great Britain. Although a number of men had toured on behalf of the antislavery movement, some remaining to study at the universities, no American woman ex-slave had visited the country since Phillis Wheatley's trip to London almost eighty years earlier. Wherever Ellen went, she made friends. "She certainly is a wonderful woman, and interested us more than either of her companions," a Welsh abolitionist wrote.

One of her first purchases in England was an autograph album in which acquaintances wrote their names and, often, a line or two of poetry. Its yellowing pages show that she met most of the greats and near-greats of the reform movement of the day. In Edinburgh she breakfasted with phrenologist George Combe and his wife Cecilia, daughter of Sarah Kemble Siddons, the distinguished actress. "She took much interest in Ellen," wrote Brown, "and was often moved to tears on the recital of the thrilling narrative of her escape from slavery." Dr. Thomas Dick, a noted astronomer, called on them at their lodgings in Dundee and invited them to visit his observatory. There the Crafts looked through his telescope while he explained the workings of the solar system. Soon afterward they spent three days with Harriet Martineau, journalist and political economist, whose books about the United States, *Society in America* and *Retrospect of Western Travel*, remain important today. A stately woman who had been deaf since childhood—friends communicated with her through an ear trumpet—she lived in the Lake Country, the district made famous by Wordsworth, Coleridge, and other poets.

Describing the visit in his book, *The American Fugitive in Europe: Sketches of Places and People Abroad*, Brown wrote: "She was much pleased with Ellen Craft and appeared delighted with the story of herself and husband's escape, during the recital of which I several times saw the silent tear stealing down her cheek. . . . When Craft had finished, she exclaimed 'I would that every woman in the British empire could hear that tale as I have, so that they might know how their own sex was treated in that boasted land of liberty.' "

During the next days, Miss Martineau drove them around in her carriage, showing them Wordsworth's home and grave as well as the magnificent lake and mountain scenery. Brown, who was an indefatigable sightseer, had already taken them to the popular tourist spots of Scotland, covering castles, churches, museums in dizzying succession, with side trips to the home of Sir Walter Scott and the scenes described in his novels. Brown was busily making notes for his travel book, but one wonders what Wordsworth and Scott meant to Ellen and William, who had not yet learned to read.

From the Lake Country, they went to Bristol to present a letter of introduction to Dr. John B. Estlin, a widower whose daughter, Mary Ann, kept house for him. The Estlins' home on Park Street became the Crafts' headquarters for the next months, the doctor and his daughter their first real English friends. Ellen's quiet charm won over her hosts immediately, although they were somewhat critical of the ebullient Brown. While arranging meetings for them in southern England and Wales, Dr. Estlin wrote to a fellow abolitionist:

We have been endeavoring to improve the tone of Brown and Crafts *Exhibition,* altering their too showmanlike handbills and securing a higher position for Ellen. She fully feels the propriety of all we have said and done and is very thankful to us. The Crafts could do nothing without Brown. He is very active and managing, but naturally wants that knowledge of English customs and society which it is important he should have, to maintain Ellen Craft in that position which she ought and might easily hold.

In letters to a member of the Boston Female Anti-Slavery Society, Mary Estlin also expressed regard and concern for Ellen:

Wherever the Crafts have been a strong anti-slavery feeling as well as warm sympathy for their personality is sure to be created. You could not have sent us better missionaries. I must not enter on any details of their visit to us or of the useful work they have been and are affecting nor how closely Ellen has wound herself round our affections and enlisted our sympathy. If I do there will be no more space for more public matters. . . .

The Crafts are "come home" to us (so Ellen has long designated this house) after a visit to several towns in Devonshire and Somersetshire where they have been doing good service. W. W. Brown went on yesterday to Gloucester and Cheltenham; they are to follow him Monday. I am longing for you to know Ellen. I am convinced you will delight in her and I hope that you and other friends will be able to help us in wisely directing their future course. I find there is a probability of their getting to London earlier than we propose being there; in the prospect of which I am not very happy; it not being apparent what means of support they will have there or what powers their friends will possess of providing for them. I think Ellen's health has never sufficiently recovered the shock of their cruel persecution in Boston to make her equal to all the tossing about she has since had to encounter and I am never so happy as when she is under our immediate protection.

When the Crafts traveled to London in that spring of 1851, they were among thousands of visitors heading toward the Great Exhibition, a display of inventions, raw materials, and fine arts from all parts of the world. Sponsored by Prince Albert, this first world's fair was housed in the Crystal Palace, a glittering structure of glass, over a hundred feet high, that had been specially built for the occasion.

Ellen and William toured the Great Exhibition in mid-June with the Estlins, William W. Brown, and other abolitionists. In addition to sightseeing, their visit was planned as an antislavery demonstration. Choosing a Saturday when Queen Victoria, members of Parliament, and the nobility would be present, the group made themselves as conspicuous as possible. They went first to the American section where "The Greek Slave," an idealized marble portrait of a young white woman, was on display. Considered shocking by some because of the nudity of its subject, the statue was the most popular piece of sculpture in the hall. The abolitionists had brought along a cartoon from *Punch* that showed "The Virginian Slave," a disconsolate black woman shackled to a post on which the stars and stripes were draped. To provoke discussion with visitors from the United States, Brown put the *Punch* cartoon in the enclosure next to the statue, "as its most fitting companion," he proclaimed. The American onlookers refused to be drawn into a debate, but one of them hastily removed the cartoon when the abolitionists departed.

Throughout the day each black visitor walked with a white companion. Ellen, whose picture in her male disguise had recently appeared in *The Illustrated London News*, promenaded through the great hall on the arm of an officer of the National Reform Association, while the two Williams escorted George Thompson's daughters. "This arrangement was purposely made," another of their companions wrote to *The Liberator*, that there might be no appearance of patronizing the fugitives, but that it might be shown that we regarded them as our equals, and honored them for their heroic escape from slavery. We promenaded the exhibition between six and seven hours, and visited nearly every portion of the vast edifice. Among the thousands whom we met, who dreamed of any impropriety in a gentleman of character and standing walking arm-in-arm with a colored woman, or an elegant young lady becoming the companion of a colored man? None but the Americans. To see the arm of a beautiful English young lady passed through that of "a nigger," taking ices and other refreshments with him, was enough to rile the slaveholders who beheld it, but there was no help for it.

After a summer in London and Bristol, Ellen and William went to live in Ockham, a village of two hundred people, some twenty miles from London. With help from Harriet Martineau and Lady Byron, widow of the poet, Dr. Estlin had raised money to send them to school there. Ockham School was no ordinary rural school, but a pioneer in what was called industrial education, an innovation that combined classroom work with farming, carpentry, and other crafts. Unusually well equipped for its day, it had a printing press and a magic lantern for showing slides, as well as chemical apparatus, globes, and an extensive library. The school had been started by Lady Byron's daughter, Lady Lovelace, when she lived in nearby Ockham Park, her husband's ancestral estate. After the Lovelaces moved away, Ockham Park was leased by Stephen Lushington, a noted barrister and antislavery advocate, and the school continued under the supervision of his daughters.

Installed in a small cottage on the grounds of Ockham Park, Ellen and William walked to School Lane each morning to pursue their studies. When they were finished with the three Rs for the day, the two pupils became teachers, William giving instruction in carpentry to the boys and Ellen taking over the girls' sewing class. "The children are greatly attached to her," a London newspaper reported, "and she and her husband are happy, industrious, and making progress in their pursuits."

The extent of this progress was attested to in a letter they wrote to Samuel May a year after their flight from the United

States. Apologizing for not writing sooner "because we, as you well know, have been deprived of the art of writing," they promised that "as writing becomes more easy to us, we will take great pleasure in sending you a few lines from time to time. And will be much pleased if you will send us the *Liberator* occasionally, so that we may know what is going on."

Their stay in Ockham provided the first peaceful interlude in their lives together—and Ellen promptly became pregnant. She kept up her studies until September 1852, a month before the birth of a son. Named Charles Estlin Phillips, after Dr. Estlin and Wendell Phillips, this "first free-born babe" became Ellen's chief preoccupation for some years to come. In the only letter in her handwriting that has survived, she wrote to Dr. Estlin to consult him about having the baby vaccinated and to ask him to send some "matter" (vaccine) to their local doctor.

As the Crafts' second year at Ockham drew to a close, the Misses Lushington offered them positions as superintendent and matron in the industrial department of the school. To the dismay of their friends, they turned the jobs down in order to open a boardinghouse in London. One abolitionist who had visited them and "their little brown baby, the first infant of the race I ever came in contact with," wrote, "Wm Craft talks of setting up a lodging house in London without capital, without much intention of drudging himself and relying on the thousands of their friends throughout the country. He appears to be so proud and secretive that it is difficult for Mr. Estlin to advise him—and Ellen defers so entirely to him that her natural good sense is lost in his folly."

In a letter to Samuel May, Dr. Estlin also deplored the decision:

William would take a lodging house contrary to the advice of his best and wisest friends. I cannot tell where he gets money even to begin. I spoke to him strongly against it. Brown talked against it. Miss Lushington thought he would not succeed. . . . Do not repeat any of this to Craft's injury; he is suspicious and selfwilled, but is really a good fellow. I fear however he must go thro this necessary business of *burning* his *fingers*. Ellen continues all we have ever found her to be.

Well-intended though they were, the abolitionists failed to understand the pressures facing the young couple. Although the Crafts found a singular lack of color prejudice in England, they came up against a class structure far more rigid than in the United States. Englishmen who worked with their hands simply did not dine with the Estlins and Lushingtons or take tea with Lady Byron. Yet the Crafts had been thrust into this English upper-class environment for which neither their background nor their income had prepared them. How was William to earn a living appropriate to their new station in life? Working at Ockham might have appeared, to some, an ideal solution for them. But William, who was energetic and ambitious, was undoubtedly reluctant to bury himself in the little village of Ockham, when London with its multifold opportunities was only twenty miles away. For three years the Crafts' British friends had been making all the decisions. Now William was eager to stand on his own feet and take his own chances.

These pressures weighed less heavily on Ellen, for gainful employment was then an exclusively masculine role. Respectable women rarely worked outside their households; that happened only among "the working classes"—with whom the Crafts, in England, had virtually nothing to do.

While she continued to have babies—William, Jr., born in 1855, and Brougham (after Lord Brougham, the grand old man of British abolitionism), two years later—William worked at a variety of occupations. After the boardinghouse failed, he imported and sold "waterproof articles," boots and raincoats made of the newly invented vulcanized rubber. Although this venture was successful enough to permit them to buy a home of their own in Hammersmith, a London suburb, William tried his hand at other work as well. In 1860 he published the story of their escape from slavery, *Running a Thousand Miles for Freedom*. The following year, when their daughter Ellen was born, he was listed as "lecturer" on her birth certificate.

In addition to earning a living and raising a family, the couple continued to take part in the antislavery movement and to meet with visitors from the United States. In 1859, when Theodore Parker came to London, Ellen went to his hotel to see him. "I count that an honor," he wrote. "She feels better now than when she lived in my upper chamber and we did not let the girls go to the street door to let any visitors in." Ill with tuberculosis, Parker died in Rome the following year, and Ellen felt as if she had lost a close friend.

Sarah Remond, a black abolitionist who toured the British Isles in 1859–60, stayed with the Crafts while she was in London. Women lecturers were still a rarity; Remond, who was born free in Salem, Massachusetts, drew enthusiastic crowds wherever she went. For the first time in almost a decade, Ellen had a chance to talk with a black woman again. She accompanied her guest to all her London meetings and entertained Lord Brougham, her son's famous namesake, when he drove out to Hammersmith to meet Remond.

Throughout the Civil War, when it became increasingly important to win British support for the Union, meetings and visitors multiplied. When Moncure Conway, a Virginia-born abolitionist, came to England as an unofficial ambassador from the American antislavery movement, he sought out the Crafts. In a letter written in 1864 he told of "a walk across a green common, then through a quiet street of the village called Hammersmith" to visit Ellen and William. "There was a pretty little girl and three unusually handsome boys. They all inherit the light complexion and beauty of their mother. We found Mrs. Craft busy packing her husband's trunk."

William, who had briefly considered returning home to join the Union army, had at last found a suitable occupation. Under the auspices of British merchants and philanthropists, he had gone to Dahomey, on Africa's west coast, with a dual mission: to promote commerce with Great Britain and to persuade Dahomey's king to give up the slave trade and the custom of human sacrifice. After an absence of almost two years, he had returned to England with his trading goods sold and a cargo of palm oil and other African produce for his backers. Although he had had less success with the humane objectives of his trip, he had brought back three boys, given to him as slaves, whom he proposed to educate so that they could be missionaries and teachers.

Now, in 1864, William was going back to Africa on a trip

that would last almost three years, leaving Ellen in charge of their household. There was money enough to manage and a servant to help with the chores, but in addition to being mother and father to her own active youngsters, Ellen was responsible for the education of the three African boys.

As the war progressed, her thoughts turned more and more often toward home. Sherman's army was marching through Georgia, freeing slaves. Was her mother alive or dead? They had not been able to communicate for sixteen long years.

Inquiries initiated by the Lushingtons, Wendell Phillips, and other friends on both sides of the Atlantic finally brought an answer from General James H. Wilson, Union commander in Macon. Maria Smith was alive, "living comfortably with some colored friends" within two hundred yards of his headquarters. Delighted to have news of Ellen, she wanted to join her as soon as money could be sent for the trip. "She is in good health, very hale, and young-looking for a woman of her age," Wilson wrote. Ellen immediately had funds transmitted to Macon and arrangements were made for Maria's departure. Traveling, ironically enough, with an ex-Confederate colonel whose children she took care of en route, Maria reached London in November 1865. An English monthly described the reunion at Great Northern Station when "an anxious trembling ladylike woman, with a little boy by her side, met that parent so dear to them, who seemed like one risen from the dead."

With the children at school now for much of the day, and Maria installed at home, Ellen was free to take part in London's political and social life. After the Civil War, the British antislavery movement shifted its emphasis to encompass black people everywhere. In addition to sending clothing, books, and farming implements to the newly freed people of the American South, the former abolitionists also turned their attention to the British colonies in Africa and the Caribbean, where, they believed, the most pressing need was to bring Christian civilization to "the heathen." The view of Africans as "heathen" or "pagans" in need of the "civilizing" influence of Westerners was not questioned by American blacks of the period generally, or by the Crafts. They readily joined in the new undertakings.

In the past William had done the talking for the family. Now the press reported that Mrs. Ellen Craft was forming a "ladies' auxiliary" of the British and Foreign Freedmen's Aid Society, was working on a bazaar for the benefit of the American freedmen, and was soliciting funds for a girls' school in Sierra Leone where the young women of this British colony would receive their first Christian and industrial education.

Welcomed in London society, she was no longer the modest young woman whose shy sweetness had won people's hearts in earlier years. She had decided opinions of her own and was willing to express them. In the only firsthand description of her from this period, a correspondent for a Boston newspaper observed her at a dinner party where she was seated next to Edward John Eyre who, as governor of Jamaica, had brutally suppressed a black rebellion on the island. Recalled to England, he had been accused of murder by British reformers because, among other misdeeds, he had ordered the execution of George Gordon, a black member of the Jamaica legislature. Ellen did not know Eyre's identity when they began talking of Jamaica, but the American correspondent reported:

Ellen knows how to use her tongue with considerable effect, and the ex-Governor was somewhat amazed to hear himself terribly castigated by a lady of whose relation to the Negro race he had no idea whatever. Whilst the conversation was going on someone hinted to her that the person to whom she was uttering her indignation was no other than ex-Governor Eyre; whereupon, frankly and unembarrassed, she said solemnly, "Do not you yourself, sir, feel now that poor Gordon was unjustly executed?" The ex-Governor, overwhelmed with confusion, turned very red, excused himself and walked to the other end of the room.

"Ellen is a kind of missionary among the grandees here," the correspondent continued:

She was the other day at a fine dinner where Artemus Ward* was a guest, and came out bluntly with "They tell me, Mr. Browne, that

*Charles F. Browne, American humorist who used the penname of Artemus Ward.

you are always very hard upon the poor Negro." Artemus, entirely unaware of the race of the person with whom he was conversing, replied, "Now, who told you that?" "Well, a good many people; but, in fact, there is a good deal in your books that would never have been written by a friend of that unfortunate race." Artemus colored considerably, for he felt that the company he was in felt a certain sympathy for her rebuke, and he said "Not at all; I abuse white people as much as I do blacks." "Well," rejoined Ellen, looking him straight in the eye, "I hope you will never again write anything which shall make people believe that you are against the Negro." Is it not passing strange that an intelligent and refined fugitive slave should be over here confronting and rebuking in high places the enemies of her people?

In the spring of 1867, William returned from Africa with discouraging news. The king of Dahomey had at first welcomed him, building him a trading house and promising to do what he could to end the traffic in slaves. He bought William's merchandise, but when payment was due slyly announced that he had no money and would pay William with slaves. Sixty slaves, chained one to the other, were delivered to William's yard the next day. Faced with a moral and financial dilemma, William chose the only honorable path. He transported the slaves to a British colony on the coast and set them free. On his return to England, his merchant-brokers were less scrupulous. They deducted the entire amount of the king's debt, some five thousand dollars, from the commissions due William, leaving him with little recompense for the years away.

Although he continued to work to end slavery in Africa, traveling to Paris to speak at an antislavery conference the following year, he finally decided to resign his African agency. A letter from Lewis Hayden told of the great changes that were taking place in the United States. Hayden was employed at the State House, the first man of his color to receive a state civil service appointment, and two blacks were members of the Massachusetts legislature. But the South was the new land of opportunity. Black men were voting and holding office in all of the old Confederate states, and there was an urgent need for experienced people there, to serve as teachers and administrators.

Hayden's letter awakened Ellen's long-dormant feelings of homesickness. All during the cold, fogbound British winter, as she nursed Alfred, her new baby, she dreamed of Georgia, a Georgia without masters or slaves. In the summer of 1869, she and William sold their Hammersmith cottage and traveled to Liverpool to catch a steamer for the United States.

Driving along the waterfront streets, she recalled the day she had arrived in the port city, frightened, friendless. Nineteen years in England had wrought great changes in her life. The bloom of youth was gone to be sure. She would never again be able to disguise her matronly figure in the clothing of a young gentleman. But she was glad to trade her youth with all its terrors for the comfortable self-assurance of middle age. And now her days as an exile were over, and she was going back to join her own people.

Home Again

Ellen and William stayed with the Haydens for seven months, "having a good time," she said. William Jr. and Brougham had remained in England to finish their schooling, but friends trooped to Phillips Street to meet the Crafts' eldest, Charles, and little Ellen, and to admire the baby, Alfred. A reporter, calling soon after their arrival, was intrigued by this family of ex-slaves who spoke with the clipped accents of the British upper class. "They are cultivated people as well as sturdy and sagacious, with much of the English manner, but with a hearty love for America which they mean to make their home hereafter," he wrote. "By and by they will visit Georgia and if they find a comfortable place of abode, will remain there as citizens."

Black and antislavery Boston were in a jubilant mood that winter. The Fifteenth Amendment, which guaranteed the vote to all male citizens, regardless of color, was being ratified by state after state; the long struggle for freedom seemed to be nearing its end. As important participants in that struggle, the Crafts were welcomed everywhere. William spoke at the Baptist church down the street when Edmonia Lewis, a young black sculptor, was honored on the eve of her departure for Rome; at a meeting of the Social Science Society, he described his African experiences. Ellen met Ralph Waldo Emerson and Julia Ward Howe at "a brilliant assemblage" in the parlors of the Reverend John T. Sargent and, on another occasion, joined with women "friends of freedom" in planning a Fifteenth Amendment celebration. Her contribution to the National Anti-Slavery Anniversary was ten dollars—just double the amount that Louisa May Alcott gave.

The annual meeting of the Massachusetts Anti-Slavery Society, in January, was a sentimental occasion for all concerned, and particularly for the Crafts, who had first been introduced to this audience twenty-one years earlier. As the society made plans to disband, speaker after speaker pointed out that there was still unfinished business in the South, where freedmen desperately needed land and education. When William reported that he and Ellen planned to buy a plantation that would serve as a nucleus for an industrial school, their project was greeted with enthusiasm.

Lydia Maria Child, a veteran of the antislavery wars who had told the story of the Crafts in her *The Freedmen's Book*, went home to collect books "and all sorts of odds and ends" for them. "William and Ellen Craft are very remarkable people," she wrote to a friend.

I send you a copy of the "Freedmen's Book," that you may read their romantic history. With funds that they have gathered in England and Boston, they are going to purchase land in their native state of Georgia, and collect a Colony of Freedmen, establish Industrial Schools, etc. They are very intelligent, perfectly upright, and have good prudence and business faculty. I think they will do a great and good work, provided the devilish Ku Klux Klan does not murder them.

In April 1870, immediately after the Fifteenth Amendment was ratified, the Crafts went South, eighteen-year-old Charles and the two youngest children with them. They left no record of what their first days back in Georgia were like, but the reality, after the cheering in Boston, must have been jarring. A small number of black people, most of them from the North, lived comfortably, but the vast majority worked for their former masters, for little or no pay. Although the new state constitution mandated free schools for all, there were none for black children in the rural areas. Even the vote, which had seemed of such significance up North, meant little in Georgia, where black men had been expelled from the legislature, and the former slaveowners were in power.

After a reunion with William's sister Sarah, in Macon, the Crafts returned to the coast. In Savannah, William went into partnership with a black man who had leased a plantation, Hickory Hill, just across the state line in South Carolina. As soon as they were installed there, Ellen carried out their plan of opening a school. With Charles as her assistant, she taught the neighborhood children by day and the adults at night. The crops did well that summer, and they might have stayed in South Carolina indefinitely, had it not been for the Ku Klux Klan.

The Klan didn't like black planters or black students or black anything—except field hands who knew their place. One autumn night, after the crops had been harvested, masked men tossed kerosene-soaked torches at the barns and dwellings of Hickory Hill. Awakened by the crackling flames, Ellen and William were able to get the children out in their night clothes, but could save little else. One-fourth of the capital that William had brought back from England went up in smoke at Hickory Hill.

For the next year, they remained in and around Savannah. Charles, having tried unsuccessfully to find work as a clerk, took over a Bay Street hotel called the San Salvador House. Ellen and William worked with him there, investing some of their own dwindling funds, but after six months they gave up the venture. By that time, they had found a plantation that they wanted to lease or buy.

Woodville was nineteen miles south of Savannah, on the Atlantic and Gulf Railroad that went to Florida. Eighteen hundred acres of fields and woodland, it had been a valuable property before the war, producing fine crops of rice and long-staple cotton. Abandoned in 1864 when Sherman's troops raided the area, it was in sad disrepair when the Crafts first saw it.

In England, Ellen had dreamed of setting up an Ockham School in Georgia, where students would work part time on

the land that their parents farmed cooperatively. But Woodville was a far cry from the English village, with its neat
cottages and well-tended lanes and gardens. Here weeds and
brambles had taken over. Fences were down, cabins and barns
rotted away. Even the main house, once a substantial dwelling,
was in wretched condition: "a miserable hole," Ellen said,
"dirty and full of rats, snakes running all over the house."

Wild and tumble-down as it was, Woodville had one big
advantage. It could be rented for only $300 a year. The Crafts
leased it for 1872 and 1873, with the option of buying it, and
went to work. Southern agriculture was not organized into
one-family farms where a man with a hoe and a woman with
a milk pail could make a living. A big plantation needed field
hands and teams of mules or oxen. Formerly, slaves had
performed the work. Now that they were free, they continued
to work in the fields for a share of the crop. But before
freedmen could be brought to Woodville, houses had to be
built for them to live in, and they had to be supplied with
work animals and tools. And before crops could be planted,
the fields had to be fenced in, as required by Georgia law. All
of this took time and muscle and money.

With logs cut from their woodlands, William and a partner
from Savannah put up fences and repaired the least dilapidated
of the old slave cabins. Four tenant families moved in and
began to till the soil. Meanwhile, Ellen attacked rats, snakes,
and cobwebs with equal fervor to make the main house
habitable. Long before her work was finished, she opened a
night school in her dining room. Seventeen people, young and
old, crowded around her table while she and eleven-year-old
Ellen gave them their first lessons in reading and arithmetic.
It was a beginning.

That fall, when they totted up their accounts, they found
that they had spent close to $2,000 and had taken in only
$115. When their partner pulled out, demanding to be paid
for the work he had done on the place, William was "pretty
well cleaned out." Years earlier, when Charles was born, Lady
Byron had given Ellen £100 in gold sovereigns. During Ellen's
stay in England, she had added to this, bit by bit, until she
had over $2,000 on her return to the United States. But this

was her money, the only money of her own that she had ever possessed. She looked on it as "so sacred," she later said, that she did not even tell her husband where she kept it. Although she must have dipped into her fund from time to time, she was not willing to risk it in Woodville.

Realizing that he would need substantial capital to continue, William went North to seek help. His first stop was Washington. Ulysses S. Grant had just been reelected president with the backing of the black voters of the South, and there were federal jobs to be had for black Republicans. Introduced to the president by a Massachusetts congressman, William applied for the post of minister to Liberia, citing his years in Africa as credentials. Although he mustered a substantial amount of support in the capital, the post did not fall vacant, and, on the advice of Vice-President Henry Wilson, he traveled on to Boston and New York. Lecturing, writing to the newspapers, and calling on old-time abolitionists, he asked for subscriptions to buy Woodville and establish a farm school there. After an absence of almost a year, he returned to Georgia with money enough in gifts and loans to buy the plantation. A group of Bostonians held a thousand-dollar mortgage on the place; the rest was his, free and clear.

Ellen had not been idle while he was away. After bringing several new families to the place, she had bought a team of oxen with which they could plow. They had raised a fair crop of rice, cotton, corn, and peas. Walking from door to door with a basket on her arm, she had bartered some of the produce for milk and grits for her family; the rest had been sold in Savannah.

The tenants had helped her to clear out a large barn for her school. "There were ten or a dozen children there," she recalled. "I had it given out in the churches that a free school would be opened, and the children came from other plantations—White Oak, Mr. Clay's and Mt. Hope. The school was opened at ten o'clock and kept till three." She taught a night school and Sabbath school, too, and on Sundays the barn served as a church for itinerant preachers.

By 1874 the place "began to look right nice," she said. A good many houses were rebuilt, the rice house was repaired,

and, with three hundred acres under cultivation, she was able
to afford a mule and buggy when she went on errands. Every
hand who could be spared worked on the construction of a
schoolhouse: a fine frame building, a story-and-a-half high,
with dormer windows that were shipped from Boston. It was
the best school building in Bryan County—and the only one
open to black people.

Brougham, back from England and a term at Howard University in Washington, took over most of the teaching. Thirty
students, ranging in age from six to twenty-five, learned
reading and writing, geography and arithmetic. A year later,
when there were seventy-five pupils on the books and "Mrs.
Craft's school" was attracting students from all over the
county, history was added to the curriculum. At an "exhibition" in the spring, one proud parent reported that "the boys
made right nice speeches and the girls read."

Although Ellen continued to teach the Sabbath school,
Brougham's presence gave her more time to devote to the
women on the place. In slavery times, they had worked in
the fields alongside the men. Barefoot most of the year, dressed
in shapeless cotton shifts made of coarse "Negro cloth," they
had swung heavy hoes and dragged two-hundred-pound sacks
of cotton to the barn. On many plantations, their meals had
been prepared for them and had been eaten out of doors, from
a common pot. Even their babies had been taken from them,
to be cared for by some superannuated "mammy" until they
too were big enough to work. With freedom, their first desire
had been to leave the fields to the men, so that they could
make homes for their families "like the white folks do."
Although economic necessity had forced most to continue to
work, they were still eager to build a family life. Finding
them ignorant of the basics of housekeeping—many had never
owned so much as a plate or fork before—Ellen taught them
to cook and clean, to cut and sew clothes for themselves and
their youngsters—"and to be good wives," she said.

Brought up under the lash, the women were hard on their
children, whipping and beating them for slight infractions.
Ellen, who had forbidden corporal punishment in her school,
was determined to stop it in homes as well. When arguments

failed, she hit on the plan of bringing the angry mothers and their youngsters to the plantation graveyard. There they knelt down and prayed until all concerned had cooled off. After a few years of her tutelage, she was able to report that "the moral character of the people had greatly improved and they were doing remarkably well. There had been no arrests for stealing or fighting and I succeeded in breaking up the habit of whipping the children."

If families fell sick, Ellen brought them medicine. She loaned one man money to pay for a wedding license, drove two young people to town so that they could be married "in style," and gave "an outfit" to another bride-to-be. When Aunt Lusitice, a hundred-year-old woman who had been a slave at Woodville, could no longer take care of herself, Ellen took her into her own home, nursed her until her death, then paid for her coffin.

While Ellen worked at Woodville, William traveled back and forth to Savannah, bringing the plantation crops to market and buying tobacco, cloth, and other dry goods to sell in rural Bryan County. A leader of the local Republican party, he ran for the state senate in 1874 and two years later represented his district at the state and national Republican conventions. A good part of his time was spent in Boston and New York, where he lectured to church groups on conditions in the South and solicited contributions for Woodville's farm school.

During his prolonged absences, Ellen managed the plantation. She negotiated with the Atlantic and Gulf Railroad when the section master wanted to buy gravel from the Crafts' property, invested in a second ox team and then a horse, and stocked the new barn with cows and yearling calves. She also negotiated the annual contracts with the tenants. Bryan County planters customarily supplied rations, housing, and seed to their tenants at the beginning of the year, exacting two days' work a week or one-third of the crop that they raised as payment. By 1875 the improved situation at Woodville permitted her to offer a better bargain, and she required only one day of labor or one-fourth of the tenant's crop.

It would be gratifying to report that the only black-owned plantation in the county became a showplace and that the

Crafts and their tenants prospered mightily. The fact is that no one grew wealthy on a Deep South plantation in the 1870s, when cotton prices were low and taxes and fertilizers high. Although more and more land was under cultivation each year, Woodville did not fully recover from the war's upheaval, and the Crafts barely broke even at the end of a planting season. The lot of their tenants improved, however. Families who had been penniless when they came now owned mules and hogs and were educating their children. Their modest success did not go unnoticed in the neighborhood. After Ellen offered a better contract, nine families quit a white-owned plantation to work for her. Soon afterward there were rumblings among the planters about those black newcomers who "lived as well as white folks."

The Klan had been broken up by the federal government, but there were other ways to injure the Crafts. One Bryan County planter sent a letter to a friend in Boston. When William arrived there in 1876, a newspaper notice appeared:

The colored man, William Craft, now here asking for money for his school in Bryan County, Georgia is sailing under false colors. He and his family live on the money he collects each summer, and not one cent of it goes to any charitable purpose. Any person desirous of making further inquiries can write to the following county offices and the above will be confirmed:—
A. J. SMITH (white) commissioner of schools in Bryan County
SHERIFF BACHELDER (white)
JAMES ANDREWS (colored) justice of peace.

William published a notice of his own a day later, stating that his son Brougham, who had received a certificate of proficiency from School Commissioner Smith, had been teaching a free school at Woodville for three years. "The whole accusation is false and malicious," he concluded.

Despite this denial, the damage was done. The mood of the North was changing. Even in antislavery Boston, people had grown tired of "the Negro problem" and were looking forward to a reconciliation with the South. When a number of William's former backers turned him away from their offices, calling him "humbug" and "swindler," he sued for libel, asking for $10,000 in damages.

A libel suit is difficult to win, at best. In this one, the cards were heavily stacked against William. Barthold Schlesinger, the man who had inserted the notice in the newspapers, was the German consul in Boston, as well as a successful businessman. His status as a diplomat enabled him to evade a jury trial and to bring the suit to the United States Court, where the judges would be more sympathetic to a man of his stature than to an ex-slave. During the eighteen months before the case came to trial, Schlesinger's lawyers scoured Bryan County, sparing no expense to find witnesses who would deny the existence of Woodville school or would testify that both school and plantation were fourth-rate.

After the denunciation of William was reprinted in the *Savannah Morning News,* Ellen found herself under attack as well. "In the first part of 1876 everything was going along splendidly," she said. "Since the latter part of that year it's been pretty warm here, I'll tell you." Not only were her white neighbors eager to tell lies and half-truths to the lawyers from Boston, but some blacks, informed that the Crafts lived on money collected on their behalf, spoke against them too. "They do not put themselves on an equality with the colored people, do not allow them to sit at the same table, and treat them as servants," one freedman stated.

While William remained in Boston, Ellen busied herself on his behalf in Georgia. She lined up witnesses also; but when she brought them to Savannah so that they could give their testimony under oath, the commissioner refused to take their depositions unless she paid him $150 for each sworn statement. When the case finally came to trial in Boston, in June 1878, Schlesinger's lawyers brought five witnesses from Bryan County and a fistful of depositions; the Crafts were able to afford only one witness and one deposition.

Ellen turned out to be William's best defense. On the stand all one morning, she gave a convincing account of the school and plantation during the Crafts' tenure at Woodville and of the money and time expended to help their black neighbors. Describing her as "a pleasant and intelligent looking lady," a Boston newspaper reported, "Mrs. Ellen Craft told her story in a plain, straightforward manner, the strength of which the cross-examination did not appear to weaken. It certainly seemed that she was a ministering angel to the people of her race at Woodville and in the vicinity."

However, when the judges weighed her words against those of the leading white men of Bryan County, their conclusion was inevitable. After ten days of hearings, they ruled that Craft was not entitled to collect damages from Schlesinger.

Although the judges had confined themselves to the issue of libel and had not found Craft a fraud, the repercussions of the trial were unpleasant. Many old friends and some Boston newspapers continued to express confidence in William, but others turned away. Wendell Phillips, the revered man after whom they had named their son, testified for Schlesinger, explaining that he had stopped contributing to Woodville because he did not believe that a man who professed to keep a school in the South should be North all the time. Joshua B. Smith, a black spokesman who had known the Crafts since their first days in Boston, agreed with Phillips. He told the court that when Craft wanted his backing to solicit money, he had asked William why he didn't go to work instead.

Either before or after the trial, Ellen made a trip to Portland, Maine, to visit Mrs. Oliver Dennett, who had sheltered her during her flight to England in 1850. Although this was the ostensible purpose of her trip, she had another reason as well. She wanted to meet the recently ordained Catholic bishop of Portland, James A. Healy. The newspapers reported that he had been born in Georgia, and photographs of him showed either a dark-skinned white man or a light-skinned colored man. Was there something familiar about his features? Calling on him in Portland, Ellen found that he was indeed the son of her half-sister, Mary Eliza, whom she had known in Clinton so many years before.

Bishop Healy, who was not proud of his slave ancestry, made no mention of their meeting in his diary, but a journalist who was boarding at Mrs. Dennett's heard the story of their encounter from Ellen and later wrote about it. In her photograph album, alongside pictures of Harriet Martineau, Frederick Douglass, Wendell Phillips, and other prominent people of her acquaintance, a page is given over to her Healy nephews, the bishop of Portland and his younger brother, Sherwood, who was a priest in Boston.

BY THE TIME the Crafts returned to Georgia in 1878, the hopeful days of Reconstruction were past. All over the South, black men were being prevented from voting and holding office. Stripped of their rights as citizens, they were forced to work as sharecroppers with scarcely more freedom or economic security than they had had in slavery days. Ellen and William were more fortunate than most black Georgians. Although the loss of financial support from the North obliged them to give up Woodville school, they continued to work the plantation with the help of tenant families and to wield some influence in their neighborhood. They were able to send young Ellen to Boston for schooling and to educate Alfred, probably in a school in Savannah. William Jr. visited them briefly, then returned to England to live, while Charles and Brougham found jobs with the United States Postal Service— almost the only white-collar positions available to blacks in the South.

In 1883 a black newspaper reported: "No colored family in the state stands higher in the estimation of the people of Georgia than the Craft family. They are well fixed in the world's goods and both of the boys are holding first class positions under the Federal Administration."

With this brief mention, Ellen and William disappeared from public view. Some time around 1890 they left Woodville for Charleston, South Carolina, where both Charles and their daughter lived. Married to Dr. William Crum, a physician and Republican activist, young Ellen became a leader in Charleston's black society and a founder of the National Federation of Afro-American Women; in 1910 she went to Africa with her husband when he was appointed United States Minister to Liberia, the post that her father had once coveted.

Living with the Crums in their comfortable house on Coming Street, and surrounded by children and grandchildren, Ellen must still have longed for her home in Georgia. When she died, around 1891, she was buried, at her request, under her favorite pine tree at Woodville.

TWO:
Ida B. Wells

Voice of a People

IN THE LAST DECADES of the nineteenth century, when black people were forced to accept second-class citizenship, one of the few voices of protest to be heard was that of Ida B. Wells. A crusading journalist who led a fight for racial justice, she started life as a slave, in the second year of the Civil War. Ida Bell Wells was born on July 16, 1862, in the little town of Holly Springs, Mississippi. On the day of her birth, Holly Springs was in Union hands as a temporary headquarters and supply depot for General Grant. Five months later Confederate raiders surprised the Union garrison and retook the town. Ida's first years were punctuated by the crackle of guns and the clackety-clack of horses' hooves as first one army, then the other, set up its tents in Courthouse Square. However, no pitched battles were fought along the tree-shaded streets, and the inhabitants suffered few privations.

Throughout the war, Holly Springs's slaves went about their tasks with expressionless faces, waiting, hoping. In Memphis,

Chronology

July 16, 1862: Ida Bell Wells born, Holly Springs, Mississippi, to Elizabeth and James Wells, slaves.

1878–83: Supports five brothers and sisters by teaching school after parents die in yellow fever epidemic.

1883–84: To Memphis to teach. Attends Fisk University and Lemoyne Institute. Publishes article about her suit against railroad for ejecting her from first-class car.

1884–91: Writes for black newspapers across the country. Buys interest in weekly, *Free Speech and Headlight.* Loses teaching job for articles criticizing schools.

1892: Tom Moss lynched. Wells's anti-lynching crusade begins. Memphis whites destroy her press. Moves to New York.

1893–95: Anti-lynching speaking tours, U.S. and England.

1895–1909: Marries Ferdinand Barnett, Chicago lawyer and editor. Edits Chicago weekly, *The Conservator;* is leader in new women's club movement. Helps found National Association of Colored Women; National Afro-American Council; National Association for the Advancement of Colored People. Four children born: Charles, 1896; Herman, 1897; Ida, 1901; Alfreda, 1904. Continues crusade against lynching.

1910–17: Starts Negro Fellowship League, a shelter, recreation and employment center for southern migrants, helps to finance it with her salary as municipal court probation officer. Organizes Alpha Suffrage Club for black women, marches in Chicago, Washington suffrage parades.

1918–27: Anti-black riots follow World War I. Wells goes to East St. Louis and to Arkansas, to investigate, report on riots; also faces Chicago race war. Lectures, presides at meetings, protests discrimination nationally and locally.

1928: Wells begins to write her autobiography.

1929–30: Onset of the depression turns her concern to unemployment in Chicago's black ghetto. Impatient with politicians, she runs for state senate as an independent in the primary, loses to the incumbent.

March 25, 1931: Ida B. Wells-Barnett dies of uremia in a Chicago hospital.

only forty miles to the north, freedmen were joining the
Union army while freedwomen worked in the camps as laundresses and cooks. When Ida was a year old, Vicksburg fell
and federal troops controlled the Mississippi Valley. Then
Atlanta was captured—and Savannah—and Richmond. Before
Ida's third birthday, Lee had surrendered at Appomattox and
the slaves were free.

Growing Up

Emancipation brought few immediate changes in the lives
of the Wells family. They continued to live in a cabin on the
Bolling place where Ida's mother, Elizabeth, worked as cook—
a famous one, her daughter later said. Born in Virginia, Elizabeth had been taken from her parents at the age of seven and
carried to Mississippi by a slave trader. Sold, and sold again,
beaten by her various masters, she had been purchased by
Bolling before the war. Her husband, James Wells, had grown
up on a plantation in nearby Tippah County and was the son
of his master and a slave woman named Peggy. A favorite of
his father, who had no children by his legal wife, he had
known few of the indignities of slavery. When he was eighteen
his father brought him to Holly Springs to learn the carpenter's
trade. Working for old man Bolling, one of the town's leading
builders, he was expected to return home after his apprenticeship was over. But the war intervened and when freedom
offered him a choice, he stayed on with Bolling, working for
wages.

His apprenticeship had given Jim Wells the rudiments of
an education and a hunger for more. In 1866 when a representative of the Freedmen's Aid Society arrived in Holly Springs
to start a school for black people, Wells became a trustee of
the school and Ida one of its first pupils. Shaw University, as
it was optimistically called, opened its doors to young and
old. Lizzie Wells attended classes with her daughter until she
had learned to read the Bible and to write letters to Virginia
in a fruitless effort to locate members of her family.

Ida's first school—its name later changed to Rust College—
taught far more than the three Rs. Its teachers, who had

come south as missionaries, hoped to create a generation of black Puritans. Teaching European history and culture at the expense of anything African, they drilled their pupils in the morality of New England, emphasizing thrift and hard work, piety and responsibility.

The lessons that Ida learned at school were reinforced at home. As the oldest of a growing family, she had many tasks assigned to her. Every Saturday night she bathed the younger children, blacked their shoes, and laid out their best clothes. On Sundays, Lizzie Wells brought her well-scrubbed youngsters to Sunday-school, winning a prize for their regular attendance. For the rest of the day, games were forbidden and only Bible-reading was permitted.

While Ida learned discipline and deportment from her mother, her father introduced her to politics. Two years after the war, black males were permitted to vote in Mississippi elections. Almost to a man, they supported the Republicans, the party of Lincoln and emancipation, and opposed the Democratic party, which was led by former slaveowners. On the day of the first election, when Bolling urged him to vote the Democratic ticket, Jim Wells refused. Returning to the shop after casting his ballot, he found the door locked against him. Without hesitation, he rented a house across the street and moved his family there. By the time the polls closed that night, Bolling had lost a cook and a carpenter—and Jim and Lizzie Wells had broken their last link with slavery.

During the years when Ida was growing up, her father was eager to know what was going on throughout the state. Barely literate himself, he turned to his schoolgirl daughter for help. One of Ida's early recollections was of reading newspapers aloud to her father and his friends and listening to their discussions. In the brief period of Reconstruction, black Mississippians served as sheriffs and constables, aldermen and clerks. There were black men in the state legislature and black congressmen in Washington. Ida was twelve when Hiram R. Revels, the first black United States Senator, moved to Holly Springs to become a presiding elder of the Methodist Episcopal Church and a part-time member of Rust's faculty.

In that same year, James Hill, a Holly Springs ex-slave and one of her father's close friends, became Mississippi's secretary of state.

In the weeks before an election, when her father paraded through the streets with fellow members of the Loyal League or attended public "speakings" on the steps of the courthouse, it was easy for Ida to believe that blacks were equal as well as free, and that she would never have to take a back seat to anyone. But Holly Springs had its Ku Klux Klan as well as its Loyal League, and in 1875 white Mississippians took up arms to drive the Republicans from power. Night after night, when her father was at political meetings, Ida watched her mother anxiously pacing the floor until his return. Hundreds of black people were killed that year, but Holly Springs escaped the worst of the violence, and the Wells family was not directly affected by it.

In spite of the worsening political climate, Ida's childhood was secure and happy. Her father, who earned a good living as a carpenter, was able to buy his own home; her mother, with seven children to care for, no longer worked in white people's kitchens. Although Ida did her share of baby tending, her main assignment was school. At Rust, where she progressed from elementary classes to the college department, she read widely, going through every book in the library. From the novels of Louisa May Alcott and Charles Dickens, and from the Oliver Optic stories, a series of popular books for boys, she formed a picture of the world outside of Mississippi—a world where good people were rewarded while evildoers were always punished. This youthful faith in a well-ordered world in which justice prevailed never entirely left her; it enabled her to keep on struggling even when the odds seemed insurmountable.

Her first test of strength came the summer that she was sixteen, when her neatly-ordered life suddenly turned topsy-turvy. She was visiting Grandmother Peggy and her husband, who had bought a farm near the old Wells plantation after emancipation. Far from newspapers and mail deliveries, they were only vaguely aware of a yellow fever epidemic that was sweeping the Mississippi Valley from New Orleans to Memphis. Yellow fever had struck in the low, swampy areas along the river before, but it had never reached Holly Springs, which was built on the highest ground in the state. Even when Ida heard that refugees from the river towns had carried the fever to Holly Springs, she was unconcerned, sure that her family was in the country visiting Aunt Belle, her mother's sister.

One day in early fall when the grownups were in the fields picking cotton, three horsemen hailed Ida from the gate and gave her a letter from a friend of her parents. The words leaped from the page:

Jim and Lizzie Wells have both died of the fever within twenty-four hours of each other. The children are all at home and the Howard Association has put a woman there to take care of them. Send word to Ida.

Disregarding her grandmother's advice, Ida Wells took the first train home. She found a ghost town, stores shuttered, streets empty, the only sounds the slow rumble of hearses on their way to the cemetery. Half of the population had fled; most of those remaining were down with the fever. Food and medical supplies were being shipped in from other parts of the country, while the Howard Association, a forerunner of the Red Cross, supplied doctors and nurses.

At home, five frightened children were waiting for their big sister. The baby had died too. That left Eugenia, the next oldest, who was paralysed and unable to walk; James and George, aged eleven and nine; five-year-old Annie; and Lily, who was only two. What was going to become of them?

On a Sunday afternoon in November, after the epidemic had subsided, a group of the Wellses' friends met in their parlor. Jim Wells had been a master Mason; his lodge brothers were making themselves responsible for his orphaned children. After a long discussion, two of the Masons' wives offered to take Annie and Lily, and two of the men volunteered to see the boys through apprenticeships as carpenters. Ida was judged old enough to take care of herself, but no one wanted helpless Eugenia; she would have to go to the poorhouse.

Remaining silent while her sisters and brothers were par-
celed out, Ida Wells finally spoke. The family was not going
to be broken up, she announced. They had a house to live in
and a little money left by their father. If the Masons would
help her find work, she would take charge of the household.

Dubious at first, the lodge brothers finally agreed to her
proposal and advised her to apply for a teaching job in a rural
school. Putting up her hair and letting down her skirts so
that she would look older than her sixteen years, Ida Wells
passed the teachers' examination. She was appointed to a
school six miles from Holly Springs, with a salary of twenty-
five dollars a month. Perhaps the bleakest in a series of sad days
came when she said good-bye to her classmates at Rust. While
they were still carefree teenagers, studying, dreaming, going to
parties, she had been catapulted into adulthood, with all the
responsibilities that the word implied.

Every Sunday afternoon Wells rode out into the country on
the back of a big white mule. All week she taught in a one-
room school, boarding around with her pupils' parents in
their cabins in the fields. Friday afternoon she rode home
again to spend the weekend cooking, washing, ironing. At
first Grandmother Peggy came to take care of the children
during the week. After she had a stroke and was unable to
work, a neighbor stayed at the house while Ida was away.

Ida Wells kept up this punishing schedule for more than
two years. Then her father's sister Fannie invited her to come
to Memphis with Annie and Lily. Widowed during the yellow
fever epidemic, Aunt Fannie had three children of her own
and was willing to look after the girls. When Aunt Belle, her
mother's sister, agreed to take Eugenia and to put Jim and
George to work on her farm, the last members of the Wells
family left Holly Springs.

"Princess of the Press"

During her first years in Memphis, Ida Wells taught in the
small town of Woodstock, ten miles outside of the city,
commuting by train instead of by mule. In the long summer
vacations, she took teachers' training courses at Fisk Univer-

sity and at Lemoyne Institute in Memphis. By the fall of
1884, she had qualified to teach in the city schools and was
assigned a first-grade class. Soon after Ida's appointment, Aunt
Fannie moved to California, taking Annie and Lily with her.
Although Ida contributed to their support and doled out
sisterly advice and sometimes cash to Jim and George, her
heavy burdens had eased.

Compared to Holly Springs, Memphis had a wealth of
opportunities for social life and for education. Captured by
Union forces early in the war, it had been a magnet for black
people from the plantations of Mississippi and Tennessee.
Most still worked as domestics and laborers, but some had
started businesses of their own and were living comfortably.
One ex-slave from Holly Springs, Robert R. Church, owned a
downtown hotel and other property and was on his way to
becoming a millionaire. The black community had its own
weekly paper; its own cultural center at Lemoyne Institute,
which, like Rust, had been founded by northern missionaries
after the war; and its own clubs and churches.

Boarding with a black family, Ida Wells was part of a circle
of earnest young people who played parlor games like checkers
and parchesi, occasionally went to the baseball park to see a
professional game, took walks on moonlit nights, and paid
social calls after church on Sundays. With the indignities of
slavery only a generation behind them, they were punctilious
about their behavior and address. Ida Wells was always "Miss
Wells" or "Miss Ida"; she spoke of her gentleman callers as
"Mr. Alexander," "Mr. Moseley," and so forth. After one of
the latter kissed her, she wrote in her diary, "I feel so
humiliated that I cannot look anyone straight in the face."

As a teacher earning fifty dollars a month, Ida Wells was a
member of the community's black elite. She attended concerts
and dramatic readings at Lemoyne. She could also take advantage of performances given by touring theatrical companies
from New York. In her diary she noted that she saw Edwin
Booth, "the greatest living actor," in *Hamlet* and *Othello*,
found *The Mikado* "bright and sparkling, with no suggestion of
the coarse or vulgar," and enjoyed *The Count of Monte Cristo*
and *The Burning of Moscow*.

More important, perhaps, Ida Wells joined a lyceum that sponsored lectures and debates. She heard the famous white evangelists Dwight L. Moody and Ira D. Sankey when they held revival meetings in Memphis. On Sundays she went to one or another of the large black churches. There she taught Sunday school and, for the first time, encountered militant preachers of her race—men like Bishop Henry McNeal Turner, a political leader during Reconstruction who was now urging his flock to emigrate to Africa.

During school vacations, the teachers took advantage of the cut-rate excursion tickets that railroads offered. One excursion brought Ida Wells back to Holly Springs where, for a few bittersweet days, she visited the cemetery to see her parents' graves and attended commencement exercises at Rust. "As I witnessed the triumph of the graduates and thought of my lost opportunity, a great sob arose in my throat and I yearned for the 'might have been,' " a diary entry reported.

Another excursion, in the summer of 1886, took her to a teachers' convention in Kansas and then all the way to California to see her sisters. Aunt Fannie had settled in Visalia, a little town two hundred miles south of San Francisco, where only a dozen black families lived. Lonely and careworn, she begged Ida to spend a year with her. Wells reluctantly agreed to take a teaching position in Visalia—and immediately regretted the decision. For weeks she weighed her duty to her aunt and sisters against the overwhelming dullness of Visalia. In September, after teaching for four days in the one-room building assigned to the town's eighteen black children, she packed her trunks and fled, taking Lily with her.

Back in Memphis, and teaching there again, Ida Wells recorded unhappy days in her diary. "I don't know what's the matter with me, I feel so dissatisfied, so isolated from all my kind," she wrote. "I cannot or do not make friends and these fits of loneliness will come. My life seems awry." Her parents' death had forced her to grow up overnight. Now, at twenty-four, she was beginning to think about the kind of person she was and about what she intended to do with her life.

Most of her friends were getting married, starting families.

"I am the only lady teacher left in the building who is unmarried," she commented in the winter of 1887. She teetered on the verge of love, yet found herself resisting a permanent commitment. When suitors came to call, as they frequently did, she would argue with them hotly, beat them at games, or impulsively send them away. She yearned for close friendships with women, then was bored with their narrow concern for home and family. Once she thought she had found a friend in Mollie Church, Robert Church's daughter, who had been educated at Oberlin College and was teaching at Wilberforce in Ohio. "She is the first woman of my age I've met who is similarly inspired with the same desires, hopes and ambitions. I only wish I had known her long ago," she wrote. But Miss Mollie left Memphis for Washington, D.C., and they did not meet again for many years.

Money was a constant worry for Ida Wells. She tried hard to live within her income and send a regular sum to Aunt Fannie—but fifty dollars a month didn't go very far, and the school board was often late in its payments. Interested in her appearance, she struggled with her conscience about buying clothes: "I am very sorry I did not resist the impulse to buy that cloak; I would have been $15 richer. . . . Bought $6 worth of lace to go on my dress and will have to pay about $4 to get it made. It will cost me more than I can afford. . . . I need a parasol, fan, and I ought to have a hat & pair of gloves but will not be able to. . . ." No matter how carefully she budgeted, she was always in debt to her landlady and to Menken's department store.

It was customary then for young men and women to have formal pictures taken to exchange with friends. Wells had her "cabinets" taken frequently, and worried over whether they did her justice. The pictures that have survived show a pretty young woman with expressive eyes, an elegant upswept hairdo that made her look taller than she was, and a chin that expressed determination.

Serious beyond her years, she was constantly striving to improve herself. Although she never intended to teach all her life, she studied "in real earnest" to get a principal's certificate. She took elocution lessons, recited Lady Macbeth's sleepwalking scene at local concerts, and dreamed of becoming an actress. She wrote a short story, considered "the stupendous idea" of writing a novel, and jotted down notes for one on which she and a friend would collaborate. She even thought of starting a chicken farm with Jim and George to escape dunning landladies and to make a home for her brothers.

"This morning I stand face to face with 25 years of life," she wrote on her birthday in 1887. "The first ten are so far away as to make those at the beginning indistinct, the next five are remembered as a kind of butterfly existence at school and household duties at home. Within the last ten I have suffered more, learned more, lost more than I ever expect to again. In this last decade I've only begun to live—to know life as a whole with its joys and sorrows."

If this diary entry struck a new note of confidence, it was because Ida Wells had found her vocation. For some time now, she had been writing for black newspapers about the concerns of black people. Her entrance into journalism was triggered by an incident that had occurred three years earlier when she had her first encounter with segregation.

During her childhood, Mississippi—along with most southern states—had had a civil rights law that forbade discrimination in public places; in 1875, a federal Civil Rights Act outlawed segregation all over the country. But by the 1880's, as black voters were driven from the polls and black lawmakers lost their seats in southern legislatures and in Congress, the guarantees of equal rights were fading too. This was brought home forcefully in October 1883 when the Supreme Court ruled that the Civil Rights Act of 1875 was unconstitutional.

"The colored people of the United States feel as if they had been baptized in ice water," wrote T. Thomas Fortune, a prominent journalist. "The Supreme Court now declares that railroad corporations are free to force us into smoking cars or cattle cars; that hotel keepers are free to make us walk the streets at night; that theater managers can refuse us admittance to their exhibitions." He proposed that black people refuse to move from first-class coaches on trains. If they were beaten or killed for their resistance, it would be for a good cause. "One or two murders growing from this intolerable nuisance would break it up," he wrote.

Six months later, Wells boarded a train in Memphis to return to Woodstock, where she was teaching. Seating herself in the ladies' coach—the first-class car—as she had always done, she began to read. She had had a pleasant weekend and the issue of civil rights was far from her mind. She was brought up short, however, when the conductor, coming by to collect tickets, refused to accept hers. Brusquely, he told her to move to the car ahead, which was reserved for smokers—and blacks. Perhaps recalling Fortune's editorial, she refused to move.

Angered by her defiance, the conductor grabbed her arm to drag her out—only to have her sink her teeth into the back of his hand. When she braced her feet against the seat in front of her, he went to the baggage car for reinforcements. It took three men to pry Ida Wells loose and to push her out of the coach when the train stopped at the next station. Bruised, the sleeves of her linen duster torn, she tumbled down the steps to the platform while her white fellow passengers stood up and applauded.

Ida Wells returned to Memphis with the sound of that applause echoing in her ears. Her humiliation was more than personal; she could not let the incident pass without protest. The same Supreme Court decision that overturned the Civil Rights Act had advised blacks to apply to state courts for redress of their wrongs. Still secure in her belief in a world where justice would triumph, Wells hired a lawyer and sued the railroad for damages. The case was tried before a judge who had been a Union soldier during the war and was sympathetic to Wells. Finding in her favor, he awarded her $500 in damages.

The case of *Wells* vs. *Chesapeake, Ohio & Southwestern Railroad* was the first to be heard in the South since the demise of the Civil Rights Act. The *Memphis Daily Appeal*, the city's leading newspaper, reported on it with a slurring headline: A DARKY DAMSEL OBTAINS VERDICT FOR DAMAGES

AGAINST CHESAPEAKE & OHIO RAILROAD. While the railroad appealed the decision, Wells, flushed with her victory, wrote an account of the case for *The Living Way*, a black church weekly. She had a simple point to make: if you stand up for your rights, you will be able to keep them.

Her article was so favorably received that the editor of *The Living Way* asked for additional contributions, and she began to write a weekly column for the paper over the signature "Iola." "I had observed and thought much about the conditions I had seen in the country schools and churches," she later explained. "I had an instinctive feeling that people who had little or no school training should have something coming into their homes weekly which dealt with their problems in a simple, helpful way. So I wrote in a plain, common-sense way on the things which concerned our people. Knowing that their education was limited, I never used a word of two syllables where one would serve the purpose." At first, her articles were confined to local news: reports of births and deaths, club meetings, reviews of concerts and plays. But soon she ventured to comment on broader issues, detailing "outrages and discrimination," deploring "the contemptuous defamation of black women," and criticizing the "so-called leaders" of her race. Before long, editors in other parts of the country were reading Iola's column and asking her to write for them.

In the 1880s almost two hundred black newspapers were published every week. A handful, most notably T. Thomas Fortune's *New York Age*, were brilliantly written and edited; most were shabby affairs consisting largely of "exchanges" from other black papers and syndicated articles from the white press, with only a page of news and editorials about their local communities. But even the poorest of them served an important function. The white press rarely printed news about black people; only through the black press could they learn about events affecting them and, on occasion, take appropriate action.

By 1886 Ida B. Wells's reports on black life in Tennessee were appearing in the most prestigious papers—the *Age*, the Detroit *Plaindealer*, the Indianapolis *Freeman*—as well as in

such short-lived publications as the Gate City *Press* and the
Little Rock *Sun*. She wrote a regular column for the *American
Baptist,* edited the Home Department of *Our Women and
Children,* and contributed to the *AME Church Review,* a
monthly magazine. When the Afro-American Press Association held a convention in Louisville, Kentucky, in 1887, "the
brilliant Iola" was elected secretary, a position she continued
to hold for many years. "I was tickled pink over the attention
I received from those veterans of the press," she wrote. "I
suppose it was because I was their first woman representative."

Black newspaperwomen were not a new phenomenon. In
the 1850s Mary Ann Shadd Cary had founded and edited *The
Provincial Freeman,* a weekly that served as a rallying point
for black refugees in Canada. Hailed as "one of the best
editors in the Province even if she did wear petticoats," she
continued to contribute to the press for many years. By the
1880s more than a dozen women were writing for black
newspapers, some doing general reporting, but the majority
editing women's columns and covering social and school
news. Since the days of Mary Ann Cary, however, there had
not been a newspaperwoman who wrote as boldly as Ida B.
Wells. While admiring her brains and ability, male journalists
invariably commented on her appearance, a practice never
followed, of course, when discussing men.

The Washington *Bee* described "this remarkable and talented young schoolmarm" as "about four and a half feet high,
tolerably well proportioned, and of ready address." "I met
Iola," T. Thomas Fortune wrote in 1888:

She has become famous as one of the few of our women who handles
a goose quill with diamond point as handily as any of us men. She
is rather girlish looking in physique with sharp regular features,
penetrating eyes, firm set thin lips and a sweet voice. She stuck to
the conference through all the row and gas and seemed to enjoy the
experience. If Iola was a man she would be a humming Independent
in politics. She has plenty of nerve; she is smart as a steel trap, and
she has no sympathy with humbug.

After a woodcut engraving of Wells appeared in several
papers, a Memphis columnist wrote,

I note that the Cleveland *Gazette* and Indianapolis *Freeman* both had cuts and sketches of Iola. The sketches were very complimentary, but Iola will never get a husband so long as she lets those editors make her so hideous. I used to see 'em before I knew her and my mental conclusion was: well, that woman certainly can write, but if she looks like that, good Lord deliver us! And I guess everyone who sees the pictures and not the editorial thinks the same thing.

While the *Gazette* editor thought that "the picture hardly does her justice," the *Freeman* said that it "flattered her," adding, "Iola makes the mistake of trying to be pretty as well as smart. She should remember that beauty and genius are not always companions. George Eliot, George Sand, Harriet Beecher Stowe and many other bright minds were not paragons by any means."

Women were so accustomed to being judged by their ability to please men that Ida endured this sexist debate without comment and enjoyed her new title, "the Princess of the Press." In addition to her article writing, she carried on a voluminous correspondence with newspapermen in different parts of the country. Their letters gave her the intellectual stimulation that she had come to miss in Memphis. Besides, friendship-by-mail was comfortably safe from personal entanglements.

Her writings brought her more fame than cash. She received a dollar a week for her *American Baptist* columns, but other newspapers paid her with extra copies and free subscriptions. She was still teaching in order to support herself when she was asked to join the staff of *Free Speech and Headlight*, a small Memphis weekly. In the summer of 1889, she managed to buy a one-third interest in the paper. Her partners were the Reverend Taylor Nightingale, pastor of the largest black church in Tennessee, and J. L. Fleming, a journalist. With Fleming as business manager and Nightingale in charge of sales, Wells did most of the editorial work. Preaching the doctrines of self-help and thrift that she had been taught at Rust, she endeavored to raise the living standards of her readers. Her forceful editorials were critical of both the white and the black establishments. Writing without fear of personal consequences, she was as frank about exposing a black min-

ister who was having an affair with a church member as she
was in attacking the poor schools for black children in Memphis. The former brought the members of the preachers'
alliance to her office with a threat to denounce *Free Speech*
from their pulpits and led to the Reverend Nightingale's
withdrawal from the paper. The latter resulted in her dismissal
as a teacher.

No matter. Traveling through the Mississippi Valley, in
Arkansas, Tennessee, and Mississippi, Wells set out to make
Free Speech a paying business. With the backing of her father's
friend, James Hill, who was postmaster of Vicksburg, and of
Isaiah Montgomery, founder of the all-black town of Mound
Bayou, she spoke at lodge meetings of the Masons, at church
conventions, and at public gatherings, soliciting advertisements as well as subscriptions. After nine months of hard
work, the circulation of *Free Speech* had increased from 1,500
to 3,500; within a year she was earning the equivalent of her
teacher's salary.

Wherever she went, she found the position of black people
worsening. Hitherto, whites had depended on force and economic pressure to keep black men from voting. But in 1890
Mississippi revised its constitution in order to disfranchise
black voters legally. Even Isaiah Montgomery, the lone black
member of the constitutional convention, had cast his vote
against suffrage—an action for which he was roundly berated
in *Free Speech*. Once, Jim Wells had been able to buy a
glass of beer in a Holly Springs saloon; Lizzie Wells's church
group had held picnics in the local park, and a fête in a public
hall. Now, new laws barred blacks from restaurants, parks,
and even cemeteries, and required railroads and steamboats
to provide "separate but equal" accommodations for the two
races.

As other states followed Mississippi's example, segregation
was becoming the rule everywhere in the South. Wells received
a rude shock when Tennessee's supreme court finally heard
the appeal of the Chesapeake, Ohio & Southwestern Railroad
in her suit. "We think it is evident that the purpose of the
defendant was to harrass," the justices wrote. "Her persistence
was not in good faith to obtain a comfortable seat for the

short ride.'' Reversing the decision of the lower court, they ordered defendant Wells to pay court costs.

In an unusually emotional outburst, she wrote in her diary:

I had hoped such great things from my suit for my people generally. I have firmly believed all along that the law was on our side and would, when we appealed to it, give us justice. I feel shorn of that belief and utterly discouraged, and just now if it were possible would gather my race in my arms and fly far away with them. God, is there no redress, no peace, no justice in this land for us? Thou hast always fought the battles of the weak & oppressed. Come to my aid & teach me what to do, for I am sorely, bitterly disappointed.

Her discouragement did not last for long. When T. Thomas Fortune proposed the formation of a national Afro-American League that would unite blacks in a fight to secure "the full privileges of citizenship," Ida B. Wells endorsed the proposal, calling it "the grandest idea ever originated by colored men. We have been asleep long enough," she wrote. "Let us march to the front and do battle."

In 1891 when the league held its second convention, Wells traveled to Knoxville to attend. Although not an official delegate to the all-male gathering, she was invited to address an evening mass meeting to explain how women could contribute to the struggle. Her speech "kept the audience in a bubble of excitement and enthusiasm," Fortune reported. "She is eloquent, logical, and dead in earnest. She should use the gift of speech God has given her to arouse the women of the race to a full sense of their duty in the work of the Afro-American League. Every woman should rally around such a woman and hold up her hands. I believe they will do it."

But Wells was concerned with arousing the men as well as the women. On her return to Memphis, she wrote a personal letter to Fortune criticizing the league because it had not taken a firm enough stand against the new separate car laws. Her letter showed that she had been thinking long and hard about ways to fight "the battles of the weak & oppressed":

We must depend for success upon earnest zeal and hard work to spread the truth of our cause. The history of the abolitionists shows that they kept up with tireless zeal, until that handful of men and women made themselves heard and people began to think. Surely we can do as much to make their work complete, as they did to begin it! But the right steps were not taken at Knoxville. . . .

As to my journey [home], I rode (as I anticipated) in the Jim Crow car; I waited (as I had to) in the Negro waiting-room, with a score or more of the men of my race looking on with indifferent eyes. Yes, we'll have to fight, but the beginning of the fight must be with our own people. So long as the majority of them are not educated to the point of proper self-respect, so long our condition here will be hopeless. One of the gravest questions of the convention should have been—How to do it? What steps should be taken to unite our people into a real working force—a unit, powerful and complete?

Free Speech continued to campaign against the Jim Crow cars until something so terrible happened that the subject no longer seemed significant. On a March day in 1892 when Ida was in Mississippi, someone handed her a Memphis newspaper. It told of the lynching of Thomas Moss, one of her closest friends.

Ida had known Tom and Betty Moss since her first days in Memphis and was godmother to their small daughter, Maurine. Moss had worked as a postman, holding one of the few federal jobs open to blacks. In addition, he had saved his money to buy an interest in a grocery store. His partners tended the store in the daytime; he worked there at night and on Sundays, checking the stock and keeping the books. The People's Grocery had been doing well—so well, in fact, that a white grocer across the street was losing customers. After picking quarrels with his competitors, the grocer led a dozen armed men to the store to drive them out. Forewarned of the attack, Moss and his partners had also armed themselves. In the ensuing scuffle, they had wounded three of the invaders.

When sensational newspaper stories reported that "Negro desperadoes" had shot white men, the People's Grocery was looted and destroyed; thirty-one blacks were arrested, charged with conspiracy. In a predawn raid on the prison, masked men seized Moss and his partners and riddled them with bullets.

Ida left for home immediately to offer what comfort she could to Betty and Maurine Moss. She arrived to find a community torn between anger and despair. "I have no power to describe the feeling of horror that possessed every member of the race in Memphis when the truth dawned upon us that the protection of the law was no longer ours," she wrote. For twenty-five years, Memphis's black citizens had been working diligently, sure that if they were educated and respectable they would win acceptance from whites. Respectable! No one had been more respectable than Tom Moss. One of his neighbors, then only a boy, still remembered seventy years later a ballad that had welled up out of the grief of the black community:

Tom Moss was an innocent man,
He was at home in bed,
Teacher of a class in Sunday School
Was shot right through the head.

Oh me, Oh my, Lord have mercy on me!
Oh me, Oh my, Lord have mercy on me!

They are roaming the streets with their guns,
Looking for us to shoot,
All we can do is pray the Lord,
There is nothing else we can do.

For Ida B. Wells, the lynching meant more than the loss of a friend. It changed the whole course of her life. In an editorial in *Free Speech,* she demanded the arrest and conviction of the lynchers—"in the name of God and in the name of the law we have always upheld." When no attempt was made to punish the murderers, whose identity was known, she urged black people to leave the city: "Memphis has demonstrated that neither character nor standing avails the Negro if he dares to protect himself against the white man or become his rival. We are outnumbered and without arms. There is only one thing left that we can do—leave a town which will neither protect our lives and property, nor give us a fair trial, but takes us out and murders us in cold blood."

There was overwhelming agreement in the black community. People sold their homes and crossed the Mississippi to settle in Arkansas. One minister led his entire congregation to California; another went to Kansas with his parishioners.

Still others, including Betty Moss, headed north. Pregnant when her husband was killed, she stayed in Memphis until the birth of a son, Thomas Moss, Jr., then moved to Indiana with her children.

Oklahoma Territory, where there was government land available for settlers, was scheduled to open that spring. In an effort to halt the black exodus, Memphis newspapers printed stories about Oklahoma's harsh climate and hostile Indians. To find out the truth, Ida Wells secured a railroad pass and traveled through the territory for three weeks, witnessing the first land rush and visiting several all-black towns. After her enthusiastic reports appeared in *Free Speech*, hundreds more departed, traveling on foot or by wagon train along the old military road that led to the West.

In two months' time, six thousand black people left Memphis. Businesses that depended on their patronage began to fail. The superintendent of the street railway company called at the *Free Speech* office to ask Wells to advise her readers to ride the streetcars again. White housewives complained of a shortage of domestic workers; whole blocks of homes stood empty. "I don't see what you niggers are cutting up about," a real estate dealer said. "You got off light. We first intended to kill every one of those thirty-one niggers in jail, but concluded to let all go but the leaders."

His callous remark was one of many that led Wells to see that Tom Moss's murder was not an isolated phenomenon, but was part of a larger movement to intimidate blacks in order to restore white supremacy in the South. "The more I studied the situation," she said,

the more I was convinced that the Southerner had never gotten over his resentment that the Negro was no longer his servant and his source of income. The federal laws for Negro protection passed during Reconstruction had been made a mockery by the white South. This same white South had secured political control of its several states [but] this still seemed not enough to "keep the nigger down." Hence came lynch law.

Reviewing the figures, Wells found that 728 black men and women had been lynched during the past ten years. Some had been shot or hanged, others burned alive or savagely dismembered. Often whole towns turned out to watch the executions and to cheer on the mob. The white press described the victims as "burly brutes" who had committed the unspeakable crime—rape of a white woman. It was necessary to kill them, a Memphis paper explained, because there was no other way to restrain "the brute passion of the Negro."

The cry of "Rape!" as a pretext for lynching had been repeated so often in recent years that even black people had come to believe it. But Tom Moss and his partners had not been rapists. Perhaps other lynch victims were equally blameless. Ida B. Wells began to investigate.

Going back through the newspapers, she found that only one-third of the 728 victims of mob violence had even been charged with rape. Of those, how many had been innocent? When the Associated Press reported that a man was lynched in Indianola, Mississippi, because he had raped an eight-year-old girl, Wells went to Indianola. There she found that the girl was eighteen years old and a regular visitor to the black man's cabin. In another Mississippi town, Wells talked to a woman whose son had been killed for raping his boss's daughter. In a sworn statement, the mother insisted that the girl had sought out her son until he had quit his job to escape her advances. When they were discovered together the girl charged rape, and a lynch mob formed. In Natchez, Wells learned of a wealthy society woman who had had a long-term affair with her coachman. After she gave birth to a dark-skinned baby, the coachman left the state.

Every southerner freely admitted that white men had relations with black women. Ida Wells had only to look at her own brown skin, or at her near-white sisters, to be reminded of that long history. "Rape of helpless Negro girls, which began in slavery days, still continues without reproof from church, state or press," she wrote. However, no one would consider the possibility of white women being attracted to black men. Yet Wells's investigation convinced her that the majority of the so-called rapes that led to lynchings had actually been affairs between consenting adults.

As interview notes and newspaper clippings piled up on her desk, Wells was aware that she was treading on dangerous

ground. Sex was a touchy enough topic; nice women didn't
discuss it even in the privacy of their homes. But to question
the purity of southern white women was like attacking God
and country. Five years earlier, a black editor in Alabama
had written of "the growing appreciation of white Juliets for
colored Romeos" and had been forced to flee the South, just
days ahead of a mob. Friends had warned Wells that she faced
the same fate—or worse—if she continued with her outspoken
articles in *Free Speech*. Immediately after Tom Moss's lynching, she had bought a pistol, determined, she said, "to sell
my life as dearly as possible." After a week in which eight
men were lynched, she had the weapon alongside her as she
began to write:

Eight Negroes lynched since last issue of the *Free Speech*, three for
killing a white man, and five on the same old racket—the alarm about
raping white women. The same program of hanging, then shooting
bullets into the lifeless bodies.

Nobody in this section of the country believes the old threadbare
lie that Negro men rape white women. If Southern white men are
not careful, they will over-reach themselves and public sentiment
will have a reaction. A conclusion will then be reached which will
be very damaging to the moral reputation of their women.

Before the editorial was set in type, Wells went east on a
long-planned trip. In Philadelphia, where she attended a conference of the African Methodist Episcopal Church, she was
the guest of Frances Ellen Watkins Harper, a poet and lecturer
who had been active in black struggles for a half-century. On
the morning of May 26, 1892, she took a train to New York.
Age editor T. Thomas Fortune met her at the ferry landing
in Jersey City.

"We've been a long time getting you to New York," he
said, "but now you're here, I'm afraid you'll have to stay."

When Wells looked puzzled, he showed her a newspaper
with a dispatch from Memphis. The *Daily Commercial* had
reprinted her editorial on its front page, adding:

The fact that a black scoundrel is allowed to live and utter such loath-
some and repulsive calumnies is a volume of evidence as to the wonderful patience of Southern whites. But we have had enough of it.

There are some things that the Southern white man will not tolerate and the obscene intimations of the foregoing have brought the writer to the very outermost limit of public patience. We hope we have said enough.

Acting on the *Commercial*'s advice, a committee of leading citizens had ransacked the *Free Speech* office, destroying the type and furnishings. Fleming had fled the city, and incoming trains were being watched for Ida B. Wells. If she returned, she was to be hanged in front of the courthouse.

Crusade against Lynching

Cut off from home and friends, her livelihood gone, Ida B. Wells remained in New York. Within a week, she was at work again, writing a column for the *Age*. Now that she was in the North where she could speak freely, she was determined to tell the whole truth about lynching. A month after the demise of *Free Speech*, the *Age* devoted its front pages to her story. Signing herself EXILED, she presented names, dates, and quotations from southern newspapers to show that the atrocities were part of a general effort to keep black people from rising. Although rape was alleged in only a minority of cases—and then not proven—the charge "has closed the heart, stifled the conscience, warped the judgment and hushed the voice of press and pulpit," she wrote. "Even to the better class of Afro-Americans the crime is so revolting that they have too often taken the white man's word and given lynch law neither the investigation nor condemnation it deserved."

The editors of the *Age* printed thousands of extra copies of the issue, distributing it throughout the country; a thousand copies were sold in Memphis alone. Black newspapers applauded the candor of the "exiled editress," and Frederick Douglass, the aging black leader, made a special trip from Washington to thank her. "You have dealt with the facts with cool, painstaking fidelity and left those naked and uncontradicted facts to speak for themselves," he wrote soon afterwards. "Brave woman! You have done your people and mine a service which can neither be weighed nor measured."

In spite of Frederick Douglass's praise, Wells's revelations went virtually unnoticed in white circles. The northern press ignored her story. The only white person to take note of it was Judge Albion W. Tourgee, a lawyer and civil rights activist who wrote a weekly column for the Chicago *Inter-Ocean*. Replying to his sympathetic letter, Wells said, "I wish to get it before the country [so] that colored men may be vindicated of the foul charge they are fastening upon [them]. Will the *Inter-Ocean* or any other white journal do that much to enlighten the public?"

An intrepid man, Judge Tourgee did speak out against lynching in his column. But it was the black women of New York who first enabled Ida to reach a larger audience. Hoping to raise money so that *Free Speech* could start up again, a committee of two hundred and fifty women organized a testimonial meeting at Lyric Hall on October 5, 1892.

The hall was crowded on the night of the meeting, as leading women from Boston and Philadelphia joined the New Yorkers to honor Ida B. Wells. Iola, her pen name, was spelled out in electric lights above the platform, and the programs were miniature copies of *Free Speech*. Introduced by Victoria E. Matthews, a fellow journalist, Wells rose to give the first major address of her career. During her months in New York she had bottled up her feelings, too intent on her message to think of herself. Now, recounting the story of Tom Moss's murder and her banishment, she was suddenly overwhelmed with homesickness. To her dismay, the tears that had remained unshed began to trickle down her cheeks. Was she going to break down and spoil this great occasion? Fighting for control, she beckoned for a handkerchief, wiped her streaming eyes—and went on.

Although Wells was upset at having displayed "weakness," the women in her audience afterward assured her that her emotion had brought home the terrible reality of the situation in the South. At the end of the meeting, the committee gave her a gold brooch in the shape of a pen, and a purse of $500. Wells wore the brooch proudly for many years. The money made it possible for her to expand her *Age* article into a pamphlet entitled *Southern Horrors*.

"It is with no pleasure that I have dipped my hands in the corruption here exposed," she wrote in her preface.

Somebody must show that the Afro-American race is more sinned against than sinning, and it seems to have fallen upon me to do so. The awful death-roll that Judge Lynch is calling every week is appalling, not only because of the lives it takes, the cruelty and outrage to the victims, but because of the prejudice it fosters. The Afro-American is not a bestial race. If this work can contribute in any way toward proving this, and at the same time arouse the conscience of the American people to a demand for justice to every citizen, I shall feel I have done a service.

After the Lyric Hall meeting, groups of women from all over the East invited Wells to address them. For the next four months, she shuttled between Washington and Boston, Philadelphia and New York, speaking on "Lynch Law in All Its Phases" and distributing her pamphlet. In Washington, where she was the guest of Frederick Douglass, her Memphis friend Mollie Church, now Mrs. Mary Church Terrell, introduced her at a big meeting at the Metropolitan AME Church. In Philadelphia, William Still, of Underground Railroad fame, was Wells's host; in Boston, Josephine Ruffin, that city's most prominent black woman, set up speaking engagements for her throughout New England. There, too, she had her first invitations from white people: from suffragist Marie Zakrzewska, a doctor who invited her to talk to the Ladies' Physiological Institute, and from such old-time abolitionists as William Lloyd Garrison, Jr. When she spoke at Tremont Temple, where Ellen Craft had been cheered more than forty years earlier, the Boston *Transcript* published a detailed account of her speech and an editorial that she thought "quite good."

There were penalties, however, for becoming a public figure. The Memphis newspapers, which at first spoke of her sneeringly as the "Saddle-Colored Saphira," now began an attack in earnest. An article in the *Daily Commercial* asserted that Ida B. Wells, "the negro adventuress," was an immoral woman, known throughout the city as the mistress of the Reverend Nightingale, her *Free Speech* partner.

Disturbed by the slur, which she felt reflected on all black women, Wells wrote to Judge Tourgee to ask if she could sue the *Commercial* for libel. Tourgee suggested starting suit in Chicago, the closest place to Memphis where she could hope for a fair trial. Although he was unable to handle the case himself because he was preparing to test the constitutionality of Louisiana's Jim Crow car law,* he recommended a Chicago lawyer, Ferdinand L. Barnett.

For a month, Wells and Barnett corresponded while she lined up character witnesses and tried to locate Nightingale, who was somewhere in Oklahoma. Barnett became increasingly enthusiastic about giving "that scoundrel" on the *Commercial* "the scoring he deserves." But before lawyer and client could meet to plan their strategy, Wells received a letter that altered her plans. It was an invitation to visit Great Britain to organize an antilynching campaign there.

In 1893 a trip abroad was a momentous event, particularly for a single woman. Wells arranged to travel with Dr. Georgia Patton, the first female graduate of Meharry Medical College, a black institution in Tennessee. Dr. Patton was bound for Africa as a medical missionary. Excerpts from Wells's shipboard log describe a voyage that was uncomfortable rather than exciting:

Sailed for England today. First voyage across the ocean. Day is fine and trip so far enjoyable. . . . Seasick. So is Dr. Georgia Patton. We have a stateroom to ourselves and lie in the two lower berths looking at each other . . . Seasicker . . . Seasickest. Ugh. How I wish I was on land.

When the ship reached Liverpool, the women parted company, Dr. Patton going on to Liberia, while Ida Wells traveled to Scotland for her first speaking engagement. Sponsored by the Society for the Brotherhood of Man, she toured the British Isles to report on lynching and Jim Crow. A dispute among the founders of the society cut short her trip, but she returned for a second visit, from March to July 1894.

*When the test case, known as *Plessy* vs. *Ferguson,* was heard by the Supreme Court in 1896, the justices ruled that "separate but equal" accommodations were constitutional. Their fateful decision upholding segregation remained the law of the land for more than a half-century. It was overturned in 1954, when another Supreme Court, in *Brown* vs. *Board of Education,* unanimously decided that separation based on race could *never* be equal.

For the first time since the Civil War, the British people opened their homes and hearts to a black woman from the United States. Unlike Ellen Craft, who had been obliged to take a back seat in public, "Miss Ida B. Wells, the colored editress," addressed audiences of thousands. Speaking with dignity and restraint, she let her facts carry her story. She had come well prepared, with newspaper accounts and personal letters from the South, statistics showing the increase in lynching, and agonizing photographs of some of the victims. As she described case after case of men burned alive, women hanged, children shot, and of the carnival atmosphere that surrounded their deaths, her listeners were profoundly moved.

Abolitionists who had known Ellen Craft and Frederick Douglass joined with women, churchmen, members of Parliament, and the nobility to form antilynching societies. The most active of these was the London Anti-Lynching Committee. Headed by the Duke of Argyle, its members included prominent reformers and intellectuals, as well as such American expatriates as Harriot Stanton Blatch, daughter of Elizabeth Cady Stanton, and Moncure Conway, who had visited Ellen Craft in Hammersmith thirty years earlier.

In Liverpool, Wells stayed at the home of the city's most popular minister. In Manchester, her host was an editor of the *Manchester Guardian*. In London, she put up at a temperance hotel, the proper place for an unchaperoned woman, until Mrs. P. W. Clayden, wife of the editor of the *London Daily News*, invited her to visit them. On mornings after public meetings, the two women worked together in the Claydens' breakfast room—whose windows overlooked Charles Dickens's former residence—going through the newspapers. They clipped the best reports about Wells and mailed them to the United States: to the president, to state governors, to ministers, and to editors. The response from the press was extraordinary. "I have quite lost track of the number of times I have been interviewed," Wells wrote to friends back home.

Wells's two months in London were a liberal education for a young woman from Mississippi. Although her speaking

(text continued on page 90)

THE VOICE

Far right:
Ida B. Wells wearing button, "In Memorial Martyred Negro Soldiers," 1917. **1:** Migrants from the South, ca. 1910. **2:** Wells, Maureen Moss, Betty Moss, Tom Moss, Jr., ca. 1893. **3:** Ad appealing for support of Anti-Lynching Bill, 1922. **4:** Wells honored at banquet for prominent black Chicagoans, 1927. **5:** Wells, Charles Barnett, Herman Barnett, Ida Barnett, Alfreda Barnett, 1909. **6:** Wells, ca. 1893. **7:** Barnett family, 1917; Ferdinand Barnett, Jr., standing, in World War I uniform; Ferdinand Barnett, Sr., Wells, seated. **8:** Poster with last photo of Wells, used in drive to give housing project her name, 1940.

IDA B. WELLS

schedule left little time for sightseeing, she met a wide range of people. A Labor member of Parliament, wearing the cap and dark flannel shirt of a workingman, escorted her to the House of Commons and interviewed her for *The Labor Leader.* Annie Besant, a reformer who had been arrested for publishing a pamphlet on birth control, invited her to address "most of the brainy women of London" at their Pioneer Club. She "was talked hoarse" at a reception at the Writers' Club, another women's organization, spoke to members of the House of Lords at a breakfast meeting, and was the guest of honor at a parliamentary dinner, where she was shocked at the sight of "high-bred women smoking with as much composure as the men."

Withal, the trip was not without its difficulties. The most familiar of these was lack of money. Although the Society for the Brotherhood of Man had promised to pay Wells's expenses plus two pounds a week, she seldom received payment and was obliged to live on sums raised at meetings and through the generosity of individuals. She had borrowed twenty-five dollars from Frederick Douglass to pay her passage over, but was unable to return it as promised. Explaining her financial plight in a letter, she told him that her sisters, "whom I have been neglecting for the race for some time," needed help to complete their education, and that she had sent the money to them instead. "I knew you wouldn't mind waiting if you knew that they had written me three times for money with which to pay their school bills."

In a second letter to Douglass, she told of running full-tilt into another crusader from the United States. Frances Willard, president of the Women's Christian Temperance Union, the most powerful women's organization in America, had been in England for two years as the guest of her British counterpart, Lady Henry Somerset. A feminist who came from an abolitionist family and was associated with all manner of good causes, Willard had made her first trip to the South four years earlier. Entertained there by upper-class white people, she had returned full of sympathy for their "plight." In an interview in the New York *Voice,* a temperance paper, she spoke of "great

dark-faced mobs." "The colored race multiplies like the lo-
custs of Egypt. The grog-shop is its center of power," she
said. "The safety of woman, of childhood, of the home is
menaced in a thousand localities so that men dare not go
beyond the sight of their own roof-tree."

The black press, including *Free Speech*, had reported the
interview at the time, but British audiences were not aware
of it. For an unknown black woman to tackle the famous
Frances Willard was a little like David facing up to Goliath
with a slingshot. But Wells had armed herself with a copy of
the *Voice*, and whenever people asked where Willard stood
on lynching, she quoted from it. After a magazine reprinted
the interview in full, with Wells's comments, Lady Somerset
vowed that Ida B. Wells would have no further opportunity
to be heard in England.

A formidable opponent, Lady Somerset cabled Douglass,
hoping that he would disavow his protegée. She also published
an interview of her own with Willard, in which both women
put Ida Wells down in condescending fashion. Wells fired
back with a letter to the papers asserting that Willard had
failed to denounce lynching for fear of antagonizing the WCTU's
southern branches, all of which excluded black women. "Miss
Willard is no better or worse than the great bulk of white
Americans on the Negro question," she concluded. "They are
all afraid to speak out, and it is only British public opinion
which will move them."

Lady Somerset's campaign might have fared better if it had
not coincided with a racist barrage from the United States.
Stung by Wells's success in building an antilynching movement in Great Britain, the Memphis *Scimitar* recommended
that Ida B. Wells be tied to a stake on Main Street and branded
with a hot iron, while the *Daily Commercial* repeated its
slander of the year before, using language so "coarse," according to the Liverpool *Daily Post*, that it "could not possibly be reproduced in an English journal." Even the northern papers were critical of Wells. Declaring that black men
were by nature prone to rape, *The New York Times* called
Wells a "slanderous and nasty-minded mulatress" who was

looking for "income" rather than "outcome" from the British. The New York *World* polled southern governors to ask their opinion of "British meddling with our affairs" and published a series of resentful replies.

"At one time I thought I would have to remain in England to defend my character," Wells said, "but the London Anti-Lynching League decided that my character needed no defense." The volleys from the other side of the Atlantic only confirmed the statements that she had been making. "It is idle for men to say that the conditions which Miss Wells describes do not exist," one British editor wrote. "The horrors and injustices constitute a sickening list, at once a disgrace and a degradation to 19th century sense and feeling," another asserted. "Whites of America may not think so; British Christianity does and all the scurrility of the American press won't alter the facts."

Ida B. Wells had had to travel three thousand miles to get a hearing, but she had focused a spotlight on "Southern horrors" that the civilized world could no longer ignore.

Organizing for Equality

As England's cold spring gave way to summer, Ida booked passage for home. "Home, did I say?" she wrote to a friend. "I forgot that I have no home." Nevertheless, she returned to the United States and not long afterward headed for Chicago, drawn there by several items of unfinished business.

She had visited the midwestern city the year before to write about the World's Columbian Exposition, a display of art and industry commemorating the 400th anniversary of Columbus's discovery of America. More than seventy foreign nations were represented at the fairgrounds bordering Lake Michigan, and every ethnic group in the United States—except for Afro-Americans. Excluded from the commission that organized the fair and represented on the Board of Lady Managers by a white woman, blacks were given only a handful of clerkships and broom jobs. Frederick Douglass, who had been United States minister to Haiti and was in charge of Haiti's exhibition at the fair, encouraged Wells to bring out a booklet which reported the progress that black Americans had made and the handicaps they faced. Twenty thousand copies of *The Reason Why the Colored American Is Not in the World's Columbian Exposition*, with prefaces in French and German for the benefit of foreign visitors, were distributed in the final months of the exposition.

Douglass wrote the introduction to *The Reason Why*, while Wells, as publisher, was responsible for lining up other contributors. One of these was Ferdinand Lee Barnett, the lawyer she had corresponded with about her suit against the *Daily Commercial*. Several years older than Wells, Barnett had been born free and educated in the North. In addition to maintaining his law practice, he was the publisher of *The Conservator*, Chicago's first black weekly. A widower with two young sons, Barnett was tall and handsome, with courtly manners and a wry sense of humor that complemented Wells's intensity. The two had become increasingly fond of each other; after Ida's return from England, they reached an understanding. She would travel for one more year on behalf of her crusade against lynching. Then she would return to Chicago to marry Ferdinand.

It was a strenuous year. From Chicago, Wells crisscrossed the country, going as far south as St. Louis, traveling through Kansas and Nebraska and all the way to California, then heading for New England and New York. Speaking sometimes twice a day, she organized antilynching societies in a number of cities. A Central Anti-Lynching League in Chicago distributed copies of "A Red Record," a carefully documented study of lynchings which she managed to compile en route.

When the Women's Christian Temperance Union held its annual convention in Cleveland, Wells made it her business to be there. Once more she crossed swords with Frances Willard, hoping to persuade the delegates to pass an antilynching resolution. But, as she wrote, "that great Christian body which expressed itself in opposition to card playing, athletic sports and promiscuous dancing, protested against saloons, inveighed against tobacco, wholly ignored the seven millions of colored people whose plea was for a word of sympathy and support."

Months later when Wells spoke in Rochester, she was invited to stay with Susan B. Anthony. The pioneer suffragist tried to persuade her to soft-pedal her criticism of Willard for the sake of expediency. Wells looked up to Anthony, treasuring the "precious days" she spent with her, but she was unwilling to compromise when she knew she was right, and she rejected the older woman's advice. Although she had always supported women's right to vote, she sometimes found her host's single-mindedness disturbing. Whenever they discussed injustice or inequality, Anthony would say, "Well now, when the women get the ballot all that will be changed."

"Do you really believe that the millennium is going to come when women get the ballot?" Wells challenged her one day. "Knowing women as I do, I don't believe that their exercise of the vote is going to change the political situation."

She was equally forthright when the head of the country's leading lecture bureau heard her speak. Impressed by her oratory, he offered her four speaking engagements a week at fifty dollars apiece—if she would refrain from talking about lynching. He even volunteered to have a speech written for her that she could memorize and deliver. Two hundred dollars a week was an enormous sum for Ida, who was living her usual hand-to-mouth existence, but she turned him down. There were other considerations besides money.

Her tour came at a time of deep discouragement for Afro-Americans. Frederick Douglass, spokesman for his people for a half-century, died early in 1895. Seven months later, Booker T. Washington, principal of Tuskegee Institute in Alabama, moved into the limelight by proposing a compromise with the South that meant accepting segregation and disfranchisement. In this period Ida Wells's was one of the few militant voices to be heard.

"She has shaken this country like an earthquake," her old friend Bishop Turner wrote from Georgia. "In the future she will be reverenced as the heroine of her race and vocabularies will be searched to write her praises in prose and poetry."

Victor-Ernest Rillieux, a French-speaking poet from New Orleans, compared her with Joan of Arc. His poem, entitled "AMOUR ET DEVOUEMENT, A Miss Ida B. Wells," began, "Tout pour l'humanité! tout pour Dieu! rien pour soi!"*

Perhaps the tribute that pleased her most was a letter from a Mississippi sharecropper enclosing a dollar:

The only thing to offer for you in your great undertaking [is] prayer and this goes up from every lip. The words "God bless her" is written here on every acre of ground and on every doorstep and inside of every home.

I don't know what is holding you up. I have been expecting you to break down for more than a year but have not yet seen any sign of your being discouraged. To note that you are a woman (I might say girl) and I a great big man and you are doing what I ought to do and have not the courage to, I think sometimes it's a pity that I am in existence.

Although the Memphis *Commercial* still referred to her speeches as "the mouthings of a wench," some people of influence—liberal editors, labor leaders, churchmen—had begun to protest lynchings and to demand punishment for their perpetrators. The number of lynchings had dropped from a peak of 235 in 1892 to 180 three years later. But that the murders continued was intolerable. Wells had hoped that a nationwide antilynching society would be formed to carry on the work she had initiated. When the group failed to materialize, she admitted discouragement: "I had done all that one human being could in trying to keep the matter before the public. I had gone from the Atlantic to the Pacific in this endeavor, earning every dollar of my expenses." Feeling "physically and financially bankrupt," she returned to Chicago and Ferdinand.

They were married on June 27, 1895, shortly before Ida's thirty-third birthday. Her sisters came from California to act as bridesmaids, and a group of Chicago women took charge of all arrangements. The bride, who had been lecturing in Missouri until a week before, was resplendent in white

* "All for humanity! all for God! nothing for herself!"

satin and orange blossoms when she walked down the aisle to meet the groom. After the church ceremony, hundreds of friends from different parts of the country joined the bridal party at a gala reception.

The conventional wedding was followed by a most unconventional marriage by 1890s standards. Although Ida had dreamed of a home of her own since her first Memphis days, she had little interest in domesticity. Since his first wife's death, Ferdinand's mother had been keeping house for him and his sons. Ida gladly joined this ready-made family and, after a three-day honeymoon, went back to work.

Shortly before her marriage, Wells had purchased *The Conservator* from her husband and his associates. Now, as Ida B. Wells-Barnett—for she never relinquished her birth name—she became its editor, publisher, and business manager. She was also president of a women's club—named the Ida B. Wells Woman's Club in her honor—that had been organized for "civic and social betterment" in 1893.

Black women had always belonged to church and literary societies, but not since antislavery days had they organized in large numbers for political action. The women of New York and Boston who had rallied around Wells in her first months in exile had become the nucleus of a new movement. During the years of her antilynching crusade, civic clubs had sprung up all over the country—in Chicago, Pittsburgh, San Francisco, Washington, and even in the deep South. The movement received further impetus when a southern journalist wrote to the British Anti-Lynching Committee not only to attack Ida B. Wells but to assert that all black women were prostitutes, thieves, and liars.

After the secretary of the Anti-Lynching Committee forwarded the defamatory letter to Josephine Ruffin, president of the Woman's Era Club of Boston, Ruffin decided that the time was ripe for a national organization of black women. Sending copies of the letter—considered "too indecent" for publication—to women's groups throughout the country, she called for a meeting in Boston in July 1895.

This first National Conference of Colored Women, whose

delegates included Ellen Craft Crum of the Woman's Club of Charleston, South Carolina, denounced the "most indecent, foul and slanderous letter" and praised "the noble and truthful advocacy of Mrs. Ida B. Wells-Barnett, our noble 'Joanna of Arc'." Organizing themselves into the National Federation of Afro-American Women, with Margaret Murray Washington, wife of Booker T. Washington, as president, and Ellen Craft Crum a vice-president, they declared that their goal was to concentrate "the dormant energies of the women of the Afro-American race into one broad band of sisterhood" and to encourage "all efforts for the upbuilding, ennobling and advancement of the race."

Wells was unable to attend the Boston meeting, but she went to Washington in the summer of 1896 for the federation's first annual convention. Accompanying her on the trip from Chicago were her four-month-old son, Charles, and a nurse to take charge of the infant during the convention sessions. Motherhood was a new experience for the crusading journalist. "I had not entered into matrimony with the same longing for children that so many other women have," she later wrote. The responsibility for her sisters and brothers at an early age, as well as her absorption in her work, had contributed to "smothering the mother instinct." Paradoxically, she rejected advice about birth control when it was offered to her on the eve of her marriage. She became pregnant immediately; Charles was born nine months later. However, although she was determined "to do my duty as mother toward my first-born and refused the suggestion not to nurse him," she was equally determined not to give up public life. Therefore, she brought the baby with her wherever she went.

At the Washington convention, the National Federation of Afro-American Women merged with other organizations to form the National Association of Colored Women. The meeting was an historic one, its participants representing three generations of black America. Old-timers who had taken part in the antislavery struggles—people like Frances E. W. Harper and Rosetta Douglass-Sprague, daughter of Frederick Douglass—mingled with women who had become prominent during

Reconstruction when their husbands served in Congress and with the postwar crop of educated women who were doctors, school principals, social workers, writers.

Ida Wells-Barnett served as chairwoman of the Resolutions Committee and Mary Church Terrell was elected president of the association, but the star of the occasion was Harriet Tubman, legendary leader of the Underground Railroad. When she came to the platform, delegates crowded the aisles, waving handkerchiefs and applauding. Still dynamic at seventy-six, she told of her wartime work as a Union scout and sang a war song in a strong melodious voice. On the final day of the convention, Charles Barnett was elected Baby of the Association, and Harriet Tubman, its oldest member, presented him to the audience.

Young Charles traveled with his mother again during the 1896 campaign, when William McKinley was the Republican candidate for president. Thirty years after emancipation, the Republican party had lost its power in the South, but it could still be counted on to take a lukewarm stand for civil rights and to appoint some blacks to federal jobs. In Illinois, where liberal Republicans welcomed black participation in politics, the Women's State Republican Committee asked Ida Wells-Barnett to join its speakers' bureau and to address women's groups throughout the state. In each town that she visited, local committee members supplied a nurse for Charles while his mother was speaking. The arrangement worked well until one nurse, deciding that she did not want to miss Mrs. Wells-Barnett's speech, brought the baby to the auditorium. As soon as Charles heard his mother's voice, he raised his own in angry protest, continuing until the chairwoman left the platform to carry him out of earshot.

By the time Charles was ready to be weaned, Ida was pregnant again; a second son, Herman, was born in November 1897. To her surprise, she was enjoying the babies and had come to feel that their upbringing, in their first years at least, was too important to delegate to others. The same sense of duty that had impelled her to initiate the crusade against lynching now led her to plans for giving up her work in order to devote herself full time to her children. A factor that may have influenced her decision was Ferdinand Barnett's appointment as assistant state's attorney for Cook County, a position he held from 1896 to 1911. Assured of a comfortable income for her family, Ida Wells-Barnett sold *The Conservator*, resigned from the presidency of the Ida B. Wells Club, and announced that she was retiring from public life.

Her retirement lasted five months, until a particularly brutal lynching took place in South Carolina. A postmaster and his infant son were killed, his wife and four other children badly wounded, by a mob of white men. Because the postmaster was a federal appointee, Ida Wells-Barnett saw a chance to ask the United States government to intervene. At a meeting in Chicago, money was raised to send her to Washington. Since she was still breast-feeding Herman, it was now his turn to accompany his mother to the capital.

In Washington, she went to the White House with a delegation of Illinois congressmen. Introduced to President McKinley, she reminded him, in her usual straightforward way, that "nowhere in the civilized world save the United States do men go out in bands to hunt down, shoot, hang or burn to death a single individual." Past appeals for justice had brought the reply that the government could not interfere in a state case. But the postmaster's murder "was a federal matter, pure and simple. He died at his post as truly as did ever a soldier on the field of battle," and it was the government's duty to punish his murderers and indemnify his family. She also asked the president for national legislation to outlaw "the national crime of lynching."

The president assured Wells-Barnett that he was "in hearty accord" with her and that the Department of Justice and the Post Office would do "all that could be done." "All" turned out to be very little. Eleven men were eventually brought to trial in a federal court in South Carolina, only to be freed by a hung jury. Wells stayed on in Washington for more than a month, going to Capitol Hill every day to urge the passage of a bill that would compensate the postmaster's widow, but the bill was never reported out of committee. As for national antilynching legislation, she would continue to fight for that for the rest of her life.

By the time Ida and Herman returned home in April 1898, the Spanish-American War was under way. Blacks in general sympathized with Cuba's struggle for independence from Spain and supported United States intervention on the island, which had a large black population. Hoping, too, that a demonstration of patriotism on their part would win them respect from white America, they thronged to recruiting stations after the president called for volunteers. They found, however, that many states refused to accept them at all, while others assigned them to labor battalions officered by whites. Insisting that black soldiers receive equal treatment—"to fight not cook"—the Barnetts and other black Chicagoans succeeded in recruiting a regiment with a complete roster of black officers. When the Eighth Illinois Infantry went to Springfield for basic training in July, a ladies' auxiliary accompanied it. The women kept the soldiers supplied with special foods, clothing, and tobacco, and did volunteer work in the camp office and hospital. Wells, who was a driving force in the ladies' auxiliary, brought both Charles and Herman to Springfield with her and remained there until the regiment departed for Cuba.

Twice more in that year of her "retirement," Wells left home: once to go to a conference in Rochester when the old Afro-American League was reconstituted as the National Afro-American Council, and then to attend the council's first convention in Washington. By that time Herman had been weaned, and Ida was able to leave both boys with their grandmother. Their absence did not prevent Susan B. Anthony, who was again her host in Rochester, from snapping out *"Mrs.* Barnett" in an angry tone whenever she addressed her. Finally, Wells asked Anthony whether she thought that women shouldn't marry. Anthony replied,

Not women like you who have a special call for special work. I know of no one in all this country better fitted to do the work you had in hand. Since you've gotten married, agitation seems practically to have ceased. Besides, you're here trying to help in the formation of this league and your baby needs your attention at home. You're distracted over the thought that he's not being looked after as he would be if you were there, and that makes for a divided duty.

No one knew better than Ida B. Wells-Barnett about divided duty, for she was torn not only between family and public life, but between the warring factions in the black protest movement. In the South, black voters were almost universally disfranchised, and Jim Crow dominated every phase of daily life. The number of lynchings was still slowly declining, but a bloody race riot in Wilmington, North Carolina, that fall had taken many lives. Discouraged by the riot, which seemed to demonstrate their utter helplessness, some blacks who had been militant in the past were now willing to accept Booker T. Washington's program. "Mr. Washington's theory had been that we ought not to spend our time agitating for our rights; that we had better give attention to trying to be first-class people in a Jim Crow car than insisting that the Jim Crow car be abolished," Wells explained.

When the Afro-American Council met a month after the Wilmington riot, its membership was split between the Bookerites and the anti-Bookerites—or, as they were then known, the conservatives and the radicals. Ida Wells-Barnett, one of the few women present, touched off the struggle between the two groups with a hard-hitting speech on "Mob Violence and Anarchy." Sharply critical of President McKinley for failing to act against the Wilmington rioters, she also charged that Booker T. Washington's policy of accommodation rather than protest was wrong. "If this gathering means anything," she said, "it means that we have at last come to a point where we must do something for ourselves, and do it now. We must educate the white people out of their 250 years of slave history." Despite her earlier support of the Spanish-American War, she now opposed United States expansion overseas, insisting that the country must protect its own black citizens before it took over Spain's colonies.

Several council members were federal officeholders who owed their jobs to McKinley or to Booker T. Washington, who was becoming increasingly influential in Republican circles. When they called Wells "hotheaded" and made a plea for conservatism, her supporters hissed and groaned. The council's final address to the nation, which was presented to Congress and the president, was a compromise statement which said that political activity was essential in the North, but in the South education and hard work would pave the way to equality in the future. Although the address condemned the president for ignoring mob violence in Wilmington and elsewhere, it accepted "legitimate restrictions" to suffrage— such as educational or property qualifications—as long as these were applied to both races.

At the close of the convention, Bishop Alexander Walters of the AME Church was elected president of the council and Ida B. Wells-Barnett its financial secretary. Secretary was a traditional woman's job, but financial secretary was something else again. The men who had opposed Wells as too radical now sought to oust her on sexist grounds. "Sentimental considerations and false notions of gallantry are decidedly out of place when great causes are at stake," said *The Colored American*, a Washington weekly:

We entertain for Mrs. Ida B. Wells-Barnett the kindliest of feelings and are not lacking in appreciation of her splendid abilities along certain lines. But we are compelled to regard her election to the financial secretaryship as an extremely unfortunate incident. She is a woman of unusual mental powers, but the proprieties would have been observed by giving her an assignment more in keeping with the popular idea of woman's work and which would not interfere so disastrously with her domestic duties. It would be productive of a high degree of satisfaction to all concerned if the executive committee could arrange with Mrs. Barnett to take charge of a national auxiliary composed exclusively of women. In this coterie, Mrs. Barnett's labors would assuredly be more congenial. The financial secretary of the Afro-American Council should be a man—the best that can be found—and one who is not barred from meeting on amicable terms the leaders of the two races, North, East, South and West.

Despite this appeal to the all-male executive committee, Ida Wells-Barnett served as financial secretary for a year, resigning then to head the council's Anti-Lynching Bureau.

She kept this post until Booker T. Washington and his supporters succeeded in taking over the council and rendering it ineffective as a protest organization. By then, however, she had two more children, Ida, born in 1901, and Alfreda, in 1904, and had once again retired from public life.

Years of Protest

During the first decade of the new century, Ida Wells-Barnett remained at home with her family. Home in those years was a two-story brick house on Rhodes Avenue, in a pleasant residential neighborhood. Chicago's small black population was not segregated then, but the Barnetts, as the first black family on the block, encountered considerable hostility. Neighbors would leave their porches when they saw them, retreating indoors with a noisy slamming of doors, and Charles and Herman were regularly set upon by a gang of white boys. When the boys chased her sons up the front steps and remained in the yard shouting threats, Ida appeared in the doorway. In a voice that carried far down the street, she let everyone know that she owned a pistol and would use it if necessary. Neither her children nor her neighbors ever saw the gun—probably the one she had purchased in Memphis—but rumors of its presence were enough to put a stop to the hazing.

Fiercely protective of her children, she was also loving and kind. She sang them to sleep when they were little, arranged Halloween and birthday excursions for them, and saw to it that they had the piano and dancing lessons she had missed. However, she was never overindulgent. Although she enforced obedience with a "look" rather than a spanking, she assigned each child specific duties that had to be carried out. She visited their schools often to check on their progress—"and the reports had better be good," a daughter recalled. Sundays were not as solemn as in her own childhood, but everyone gathered around the dining table to read the Bible together before going off to Sunday school and church. Afterwards they paid calls, visiting Ida's sister, Annie, who had married a Chicagoan, or going to see Grandmother Barnett and their half-brothers, who had moved to an apartment before Alfreda's birth.

Despite her devotion to her children, Ida did not allow herself to be swamped by housekeeping chores. There was always someone, a cousin from the South or a day-worker, to do the laundry and cleaning. Ferdinand, who enjoyed cooking, prepared the evening meals. "Mother was very displeased by the fact that if you swept the house today, tomorrow you had to do the same thing," her daughter, Alfreda M. Duster, explained. "She didn't feel that she was *accomplishing* anything."

Throughout the years of her "retirement," Ida Wells's professional and political activities continued. Seated at the dining table surrounded by newspapers and magazines, she wrote steadily: a pamphlet on "Mob Rule in New Orleans" after a lynching there, articles for such influential publications as *World Today* and *Independent,* and endless letters to the newspapers. No week went by without a meeting of some sort. She addressed white organizations to urge school integration when segregation was threatened or to describe the employment problems of black women. In addition to her work with the Ida B. Wells Club, in which she continued to be a leader, she was vice-president of the interracial Douglass Women's Club; founder of an Afro-American Historical Society; and a backer of the Pekin Theatre, where many talented black actors and musicians received their first opportunity to perform.

In 1909 Wells went to New York for the founding conference of the National Association for the Advancement of Colored People, in the hope that it would become the fighting organization that the Afro-American Council had once promised to be. On the opening day of the conference, she gave an eloquent report on the 3,284 people who had been lynched during the past quarter of a century. "Why is mob murder permitted by a Christian nation? What is the cause of this awful slaughter?" she asked. To refute the "shameless falsehood that 'Negroes are lynched to protect womanhood,' " she cited hundreds of instances in which men and women were killed for such "crimes" as practicing voodoo, killing a horse, keeping a saloon, or quarreling with a white man.

After the speeches were over, the conference met to draw up a program for action. Most of the people in attendance were white liberals, distinguished professionals who were sincere in their desire to help blacks win equality, but who were not always free from racial bias. Fearing that the program would not be militant enough, a small group of blacks, including Wells, attempted to strengthen the organization's statement of purpose and to add some resolutions of their own, among them a plea to make lynching a federal crime. Although the final statement was a strongly-worded one that demanded of Congress and the president "that the Constitution be strictly enforced and the civil rights guaranteed under the 14th amendment be secured impartially to all," the anti-lynching proposal failed to pass. Describing the stormy session which lasted past midnight, W. E. B. DuBois, who became the association's only black officer, reported that a woman, undoubtedly Ida Wells, "leapt to her feet and cried in passionate, almost tearful earnestness—an earnestness born of bitter experience—'They are betraying us again—these white friends of ours.' "

When a Committee of Forty was appointed to form a permanent organization, Wells and the other black militants were left out. So many whites objected to this, offering to resign in order to make room for her, that her name was quickly added to the roster. The incident continued to rankle, however. She never overcame the feeling that some of her white colleagues were patronizing her and attempting to keep control of the association. After several years on the executive committee, she resigned when its chairman called a meeting in Chicago without notifying her.

The Barnetts often worked together as a team in the fight for justice. As assistant state's attorney, Ferdinand Barnett was in a position to know what was happening throughout Illinois. When his official position prevented him from taking action, Ida Wells-Barnett went forth to do battle in his stead. In the fall of 1909, a lynching in Cairo, Illinois, aroused black

Chicago. A state law required the governor to suspend the sheriff who had permitted the lynching to take place, but the sheriff had petitioned for reinstatement. And it seemed likely that he would receive it, Ferdinand reported one evening at supper, unless someone opposed him. Ferdinand had spent a fruitless afternoon trying to find a man to appear at the hearing before the governor.

"And so it would seem that you will have to go to Cairo," he concluded his conversation with Ida. "Your train leaves at eight o'clock."

For once, Ida resisted the assignment. "I had been accused by some of our men of jumping in ahead of them and doing work without giving them a chance," she recalled. Besides, she had appointments for the next days, and it was inconvenient for her to leave.

While Ferdinand wisely retreated behind his evening paper, thirteen-year-old Charles joined the conversation. "Mother," he said, "if you don't go, nobody else will."

If you don't go, nobody else will. Ida had responded to that call all her life. It was too late for the evening train, but the next morning all four children and their father escorted her to the station. She spent three days in Cairo where she visited the scene of the lynching, interviewed eyewitnesses, and read newspaper accounts of the crime; then she went on to Springfield.

At the hearing in the capital, the cards seemed stacked against her. The sheriff was accompanied by leading citizens of Cairo, all of them political supporters of the governor. His parish priest sat beside him while his lawyer, a state senator, read telegrams and letters of endorsement from judges, ministers, club women, and even from some black people. The Barnetts had assumed that the attorney general would argue the case against the sheriff. Instead, when the defense lawyer finished, the governor announced that "Mrs. Barnett is here to represent the colored people of Illinois." She was to carry the burden of the opposition alone.

After reading a legal brief that Ferdinand had prepared, she presented the evidence she had collected in Cairo. Speaking for more than four hours, she proved that the sheriff had known beforehand of the planned lynching, but had failed to take steps to prevent it. In conclusion, she urged the governor to reject the sheriff's petition for reinstatement because "it will mean an encouragement to mob violence." To the surprise of all political observers, the governor ruled that the sheriff had not properly protected his prisoner. His refusal to reinstate the sheriff served as a warning to other police officers, and there were no more lynchings in Illinois.

The black population of Chicago had almost tripled since Ida Wells had moved there. Fleeing near-starvation conditions in the South, thousands of sharecroppers and tenant farmers were arriving in the city every year. Although settlements like Jane Addams's Hull House lent a helping hand to newly-arrived immigrants from Europe, few social services were available for these southern migrants, who were equally ill-prepared for urban life. The older migrant women were usually able to find day work to augment their income, while the younger ones took live-in domestic jobs. But there was less work available for the men, particularly the teenagers and young adults. Turned away from factory gates and union hiring halls and barred from the dormitories and recreational facilities of the YMCA or the Salvation Army, they found a welcome only in the saloons, poolrooms, and gambling houses of Chicago's crowded South Side.

Disturbed by the growing crime rate among the newcomers, Wells appealed to the young men in a Bible class she taught on Sundays. At her suggestion, they started a social center in a storefront on State Street, in the heart of the ghetto. The Negro Fellowship League Reading Room and Social Center opened its doors in 1910. Its first floor was fitted out with hometown papers, books, games, and a piano; upstairs was a dormitory where the "men farthest down and out" could find lodging for fifteen cents a night. For three years, a white couple paid the rent and the salary of a secretary who ran an employment office, but Ida Wells was at the center every day to counsel new arrivals. Sometimes she brought home a boy who was sick or who had gotten into trouble, taking care of him until he was on his own again.

Most of the regulars at the center were men, but women

came to the employment office to find jobs. While they waited
for assignments as laundresses or cooks, Wells took the opportunity to talk with them, sometimes tactfully suggesting
that they give up rural ways of dressing and behavior. One
down-home custom that offended Chicagoans was the wearing
of boudoir caps on the street. Wells's quiet campaign against
the caps was so successful that, decades later, a public speaker
gave her credit for their disappearance.

She was in the office one day when a frightened twenty-
three-year-old was brought in. Held in virtual slavery by a
white family, she had worked for them without pay since
childhood. After her mistress attempted to beat her, the young
woman had summoned up the courage to run away, but she
was too intimidated to return to her former home to collect
her belongings.

Wells promptly called on her "employer," announcing that
she had come to get the girl's clothes and to place her in
more congenial surroundings. "I told her that since she had
had the girl's labor with no remuneration, steps would be
taken to see that she got what was due her." When the
white woman heard this, she was immediately conciliatory.
Not only did she give the young woman her clothes, but she
paid her some seven hundred dollars in back wages. It was
"a very pleasant interview, all things considered," Wells recalled.

The police were hard on the young male migrants, arresting
them often and railroading them to prison for crimes they
had not committed. Wells was soon a familiar figure in the
courts where, with Ferdinand's help, she defended the wrong-
fully accused or sought light sentences for the guilty. When
the couple who had been financing the league withdrew their
support, she secured a position as probation officer—the first
black woman to receive such an appointment—and used her
salary of one hundred fifty dollars a month to carry on the
league's activities. On duty in the municipal court from nine to
five, she spent most evenings at the center working with pa-
rolees. By this time her older children were almost grown and
even ten-year-old Alfreda was in school. Ida kept in touch with

her by telephone, calling her when she came home for lunch, to remind her to eat properly and to leave in time for her afternoon classes.

When a new city administration came to power in 1916, Wells lost her court appointment. After that, it was an uphill struggle to keep the Fellowship League going. Few middle-class blacks shared her interest in the down-and-outers of State Street, preferring instead to contribute to more respectable organizations like the new Urban League and the all-black Y that had finally been built on the South Side. Wells's support came from working people—an elevator operator, a railroad-station porter, a ragpicker who turned up on Sundays to lead the center's Bible class—but it was difficult to meet expenses. At last, in 1920, when the center was four months behind with the rent and the man in charge of the employment office had decamped, taking the furniture with him, she reluctantly closed its doors.

Throughout her years on State Street, Wells kept up her political activities. She had been a member of the white-led Women's Suffrage Association since her first days in Chicago. When the Illinois legislature gave women the vote in local elections, she formed the Alpha Suffrage Club, the state's first suffrage organization for black women. In the predominantly black Second Ward, club members canvassed from house to house, urging women to register so that they could use their votes to elect a black alderman to the city council. Men jeered at them, telling them to go home and take care of their babies. But the women were so successful in getting out the vote that politicians soon came to their meetings to ask for support, and the Second Ward elected its first black alderman the following year.

The black suffragists marched with the whites when they paraded down Michigan Avenue in Chicago to urge the passage of a federal suffrage amendment. Dressed in white, with streamers proclaiming "Alpha Suffrage Club," Alfreda accompanied her mother on that occasion. Several months later, Wells went to Washington, one of five thousand women converging on the capital to demand the vote. A gigantic

parade up Pennsylvania Avenue was to climax the demonstrations, but Wells was told by officers of the National American
Woman Suffrage Association that she must not join it, lest
her dark-skinned presence antagonize southern white women.
Backed by the Illinois delegation, she marched anyway. An
admirer commemorated the incident with a rhyme beginning:

Side by side with the whites she walked,
Step after step the Southerners balked,
But Illinois, fond of order and grace,
Stuck to the black Queen of our race.

The suffrage parade took place in 1913, on the eve of
Woodrow Wilson's inauguration. Eight months afterwards,
Wells was back in Washington, this time as a member of the
executive committee of the National Equal Rights League,
an organization which boasted that it was "of the colored
people, for the colored people and led by the colored people."
The league had been founded by William Monroe Trotter, a
leader of the opposition to Booker T. Washington. Wells and
Trotter had worked together at the founding conference of
the NAACP four years earlier; they were joining forces now
to present a protest to the president. Wilson, the first Democrat to occupy the White House in twenty years, had confirmed
black people's forebodings by appointing five southerners to
his cabinet. They in turn had segregated the employees in
their departments, forbidding blacks to share the restaurants
and rest rooms used by whites.

The president listened courteously when the league delegation asked him to halt this new segregation, but he did
nothing to change the situation. A year later Trotter returned
to the White House, only to hear Wilson defend segregation
as "a benefit" for black people, rather than "a humiliation."
When Trotter attempted to argue with him, Wilson called
him insolent and refused to meet with him again. The Wilson-
Trotter confrontation made front-page headlines the next day,
thereby giving the segregation issue the widest possible publicity. Wells had been unable to accompany Trotter on this
second trip, but she showed her support of him by inviting

him to visit her in Chicago and arranging speaking engagements for him throughout the Midwest.

After the United States entered World War I, Wells had her own confrontation with the government. In August 1917, black soldiers in Houston, Texas, goaded beyond endurance by local citizens, turned on their tormentors, killing a number of whites. Following a summary court martial that allowed no appeal, nineteen soldiers were hanged; scores more were sentenced to life imprisonment. Shocked by the speed and severity of the punishment, Wells planned a memorial service for the dead men. To publicize the meeting, she had some buttons made up that said, "In Memorial MARTYRED NEGRO SOLDIERS." After she gave one to a reporter, she had a visit from two Secret Service men. They warned her that she would be arrested if she gave out the buttons.

"On what charge?" she asked.

"Treason," one said.

"You've criticized the government," his partner added.

"And the government deserves to be criticized," Wells promptly replied. "If it is treason for me to think and say so, then you will have to make the most of it."

They had hoped to intimidate her, but when she refused to give up the buttons, challenging them to arrest her, they departed, muttering threats. Years later she still wore a button honoring the martyred soldiers. *

The violence in Houston was soon overshadowed by a series of race riots in northern cities. The wartime boom had brought half a million black people to the North to work in mills and factories. Fearing competition for jobs and housing, white workers turned on the newcomers with increasing fury. A month before the outbreak in Houston, Wells had traveled to East St. Louis, Illinois, where more than forty blacks had been killed in a riot and thousands had been driven from their homes. Alone, with no credentials except a sense of outrage, she got off the train three days after the fighting had subsided,

* After two decades of protests, the last of the Houston prisoners was pardoned by President Franklin D. Roosevelt in 1938.

the first investigator to tour the burned-out neighborhoods and interview survivors. From East St. Louis she went to Springfield for an interview with the governor. When she told him that National Guardsmen had stood by while the mob murdered blacks, he promised a sweeping investigation if she would line up witnesses.

Wells went back to East St. Louis, only to find that federal investigators who had arrived on the scene were focusing their attention not on the instigators of the riot, but on a group of black men who had organized to defend themselves. The white men and women responsible for the riot were given short prison terms, but eleven blacks were convicted of murder. Outraged at this miscarriage of justice, Wells made still a third trip to East St. Louis to collect facts on which an appeal could be based. A series of articles she wrote for the Chicago *Defender* helped mobilize public sentiment. The leader of the group, who had been sentenced to life imprisonment, was freed by the Illinois Supreme Court; the others were pardoned by the governor after years in the penitentiary.

In 1918, when Ida was fifty-six, the Barnetts moved to a fine eight-room house on Chicago's Grand Boulevard. Formerly a mansion owned by wealthy whites, it had parquet floors, marble sinks, and a third-floor ballroom that they converted into an apartment for their son, Herman, and his wife, Fione. Their enjoyment of their new home was marred, however, by the attitude of white property owners who vowed to stop the black "invasion" of their neighborhood "at all cost." After a series of bombings of black residences on and near Grand Boulevard, Wells foresaw disaster. In a letter to the Chicago *Tribune,* she implored city officials "to set the wheels of justice in motion before it is too late and Chicago be disgraced by the bloody outrages that have disgraced East St. Louis."

Three weeks later a clash between white and black youngsters escalated into a full-scale race war. For five days armed mobs took over the city, beating, killing, burning. When the final casualty figures were in, twenty-three blacks and fifteen whites were dead and more than five hundred seriously injured. While all sensible people, including her husband and children, stayed indoors, Wells was out in the streets day and night to organize a Protective Association and to find out what was happening for the investigation that was sure to follow.

Chicagoans were still cleaning up their debris when news came of a massacre in Arkansas. After sharecroppers in rural Phillips County met to organize a union, armed whites from as far away as Tennessee and Mississippi poured into the area, killing indiscriminately. The response of the forces of law and order was to arrest hundreds of black men and women. Herded into a stockade where they were kept virtually incommunicado, these "black revolutionists," as they were called, were charged with conspiring to murder whites and seize their lands. After a trial lasting less than an hour, sixty-seven blacks received long prison terms, and twelve were condemned to death.

The case dragged on for years. Three times gallows were built for the convicted men; three times last-minute pleas to higher courts saved their lives. Wells interested herself in their fate from the beginning, calling protest meetings and appealing, through the columns of the *Defender*, for money for their defense. However, in the concentration camp atmosphere that still prevailed in Phillips County, it was difficult to ascertain the facts. One NAACP investigator who had posed as a white newspaperman barely escaped lynching when he tried to interview the prisoners.

At last, Ida Wells decided to go to Arkansas herself. Arriving in Little Rock on a Sunday morning in January 1922—her first trip to the South in thirty years—she went directly to the home of one of the condemned men's wives. That afternoon when the women visited their husbands, the prison guards scarcely noticed the plump, gray-haired woman accompanying them who was introduced as a cousin from St. Louis. But the prisoners' eyes lit up as the women, drawing close to their cells, managed to whisper that this "cousin" was Ida Wells-Barnett from Chicago.

Talking in undertones, Wells asked for details of the massacre and of the torture the prisoners had been subjected to when first arrested. She also collected information about the size of their farms, the crops raised, and the number of cattle and hogs they had owned—for they had lost everything they had spent a lifetime working for.

When the men tired of talking, they began to sing—songs of their own composition and old spirituals—while their wives took up the refrains. Wells listened thoughtfully to the singing, then approached the cells again. In an urgent whisper, she remonstrated with the men:

You have sung and prayed about dying, and forgiving your enemies and of feeling sure that you are going to the New Jerusalem because your God knows that you are innocent. But why don't you pray to live and ask to be freed? The God you serve is the God of Paul and Silas who opened their prison gates. You ought to believe that he will open your prison too.

If you do believe that, let your songs be songs of faith and hope; that the judges who pass on your cases will be given the wisdom and courage to decide in your behalf. Quit talking about dying. Pray to live and believe you are going to get out.

Unable to take notes while in the prison, Wells spent most of the night putting down the information that the men, and the women who had been imprisoned earlier, had given her. After talking with the prisoners' lawyer and the local committee that was raising money for their defense, she returned to Chicago to write a pamphlet, *The Arkansas Race Riot,* so that the whole country could know the truth about the sharecroppers from Phillips County. At last, in 1923, the Supreme Court ruled that the men had not had a fair trial; over the next years all of the prisoners were set free.

VIGOROUS IN HER SIXTIES—"she walked like she owned the world," her daughter said—Ida Wells-Barnett presided over meetings, lectured, collected signatures on petitions, and fought a rising tide of discrimination in Chicago. Once, when she was shopping in a Loop department store, a salesclerk refused to wait on her. Head high, with her would-be purchase dangling over her arm, she marched toward an exit. After a floorwalker stopped her, she paid for the purchase, and went home to write a letter to the papers reporting the incident.

Slowing down only imperceptibly, Wells allowed herself leisure to enjoy her grandchildren and to visit her sisters. She had no close friends. There had never been time for casual conversations, for luncheons and dinner parties. The women who called—and there were many callers—were intent on business: an agenda for a meeting, raising funds, preparing publicity. As the depression cut into Ferdinand's income and her own lecture fees dwindled, the Barnetts moved from the Grand Boulevard house to a small apartment. In the evenings Ida and Ferdinand went to the movies together or set up a card table for a game of whist while the Victrola played Caruso records.

She was as interested as ever in politics. By 1929, Chicago's blacks had six representatives in the state legislature and one in Congress—the first black congressman in Washington since Reconstruction. Over the years, however, Wells had learned that a "first" black alderman or a "first" black congressman was not enough. Elected officials ought to be dedicated people with a concern for the welfare of their constituents, but unfortunately Chicago's black representatives were usually machine politicians, in a city where the machines were notoriously corrupt. They did favors for their supporters, but made little effort to improve conditions in their district. Unemployment had always been high on Chicago's South Side; with the depression, blacks were the first fired and the first to be evicted from their homes. Encountering hungry, homeless people on the streets, Wells felt that more needed to be done than the legislators were doing. At the age of sixty-seven, she decided to run for the state senate.

Wells and her husband had always been registered Republicans,* affiliated with the liberal wing of the party. When neither the liberals nor the regulars would endorse Wells's candidacy, she ran in the Republican primary as an independent. Most of her support came from women, her associates

---

*Blacks remained loyal to the Republican party until President Franklin D. Roosevelt instituted his New Deal reforms in the mid-thirties. In 1932 seventy-seven percent of Chicago's black voters cast their ballots for Herbert Hoover, the Republican presidential candidate.

in half a dozen organizations, who circulated her nominating petitions, gave out leaflets, and put placards in store windows. She traveled to churches and club meetings, often speaking twice a day on her own behalf. In the three-cornered race, she was not surprised when the incumbent was declared the victor. "He would be, with the machine behind him which always wins," she wrote. "The independent vote is weak, unorganized and its workers purchasable." And, because no one ever measured up to the standards she set for herself, she was disappointed that "few women responded as I had hoped."

Wells was working on her autobiography in those years. Occasionally, as she wrote, this same note of disappointment crept in. Always impatient with the "do-nothings," she had forged ahead alone. Sometimes her boldness had alienated people so that others, more willing to compromise, had received the recognition that could have been hers. In 1924 she had run for the presidency of the National Association of Colored Women, hoping to reshape it into the dynamic organization that it had at first promised to be, but she had lost out to a younger woman who was better schooled in diplomacy. Had she been more moderate in her views and in her expression of them, she might have played a leadership role in the NAACP, which had taken up her fight for a federal antilynching law and was meeting with some success in Washington.

Still, she had few regrets. Looking back over a lifetime of struggle, she could say that she had shared the action and passion of her time as no other black woman and few men had done. For forty years, she had been in the forefront of the fight for equality, for justice, and for human dignity. Writing, speaking, spurring others on, she had told the truth in words so stirring that she had forced the world to listen. True, each hard-fought victory had led to another struggle. There remained endless hurdles for her people to surmount—but some day they would win.

She was warning that vigilance was needed to preserve "our rights" when her autobiography broke off in mid-sentence. Her pen lay on a table still heaped high with books and magazines—but Ida B. Wells was dead.

Her death occurred on March 25, 1931, four months before her sixty-ninth birthday. She was not forgotten. In 1940, when the federal government built the first low-cost housing project in Chicago's black belt, the Ida B. Wells Woman's Club spearheaded a drive to name the project in her honor. Visitors to Chicago can still see the Ida B. Wells Homes, well-kept garden apartments that house some seven thousand tenants. And diagonally across the street, on what is now Martin Luther King Drive, her Grand Boulevard residence bears a plaque, placed there by the Department of the Interior, that designates the Ida B. Wells-Barnett House as a National Historic Landmark.

THREE:
Mary Church Terrell

Ninety Years for Freedom

"IF IT HADN'T BEEN FOR THE VICTORY of the Union Army," Mary Church Terrell often said, "I should be on some plantation in the South, manacled body and soul in the fetters of a slave." The statement was true, as far as it went. Mary Church was born of slave parents shortly before the end of the Civil War; neither parent, however, had known the hardships of plantation life.

Mary Church's father, Robert Reed Church, was the son of Captain Charles B. Church of Holly Springs, Mississippi, and a slave maidservant, Emmeline. Separated from his mother when her owners moved further west, Robert was brought up by his father, who was genuinely fond of his slave son and gave him everything he wanted—except freedom. Captain Church owned a line of Mississippi River boats. As a youth, Robert worked on his father's boats, first as a dishwasher, then as steward in charge of purchasing. He was twenty-four when Union gunboats wrested control of the river from the Confed-

Chronology

September 23, 1863: Mary Eliza Church born, Memphis, Tennessee, to newly-emancipated Louisa and Robert Reed Church.

Ca. 1868: Churches divorce. Mary Eliza (known as Mollie) and younger brother, Thomas, live with their mother.

1884–90: Graduates Oberlin College; teaches at Wilberforce University, then at Washington, D.C. high school. Studies abroad for two years, returns to Washington to teach again.

1891: Marries Robert Terrell, teacher and lawyer, who later is a judge of the Municipal Court in District of Columbia.

1892–98: Elected president of National Association of Colored Women. First black woman appointed to D.C. Board of Education. Has four babies; a daughter, Phyllis, survives.

1898–1905: Addresses convention of National American Woman Suffrage Association. In Berlin, addresses International Council of Women. Adopts niece, Mary Church.

1905–17: Lectures, writes on black life and history; is a founder of National Association for the Advancement of Colored People; joins suffragists picketing White House.

1919–25: As delegate to International Congress of Women at Zurich, she speaks on condition of black Americans. Receives Republican National Committee appointment as director of Work among Colored Women in the East. Widowed in 1925.

1929–40: Directs organization of black voters in Republican campaigns, including Herbert Hoover's. Publishes autobiography, *A Colored Woman in a White World.*

1946–50: With honorary degrees from three institutions, wages successful fight to open membership in American Association of University Women to minority women. Pleads case of Rosa Ingram before United Nations.

1950–53: Heads Coordinating Committee for the Enforcement of D.C. Anti-Discrimination Laws. Pickets, leads delegations, is key witness in test case which reaches Supreme Court. Justices rule that D.C. restaurants must serve all.

1953: On ninetieth birthday, 700 gather to honor her. She leads delegation to Georgia, seeking Rosa Ingram parole.

July 24, 1954: Dies at her summer home in Maryland.

erates and put the Captain's packet line out of business. Set-
tling in Memphis, which was then in Union hands, young
Church bought a saloon on De Soto Street, and courted Louisa
Ayres.

Louisa was also relatively fortunate. A lady's maid in the
Ayres household, where her mother was housekeeper, she was
taught to read and write, in violation of the law, and even given
French lessons. When she agreed to marry Robert Church, her
master provided her with a trousseau from New York and an
elegant wedding reception. After the Emancipation Proclamation freed the young couple, Louisa opened a "hair store" where
Memphis's wealthiest ladies flocked to buy curls and chignons
and to have their hair coiffed for important occasions. The
store was so successful that Louisa's earnings paid for the
Churches' first home and carriage.

When the Churches' daughter, Mary Eliza, was born on
September 23, 1863, victory for the Union Army was still a year
and a half away, and Memphis was overflowing with black
refugees from the war-torn countryside. Men and women
crowded into ramshackle dwellings near the river and earned
a precarious living working for the army. Mollie Church, as
she was always called, grew up in a world apart from these
ragged, hungry, newly freed people. Her first years were spent
in a suburb of the city; and her first playmates were white.
When she was small, her father used to take her on Sunday
visits to Captain Church. The older man would greet her affec-
tionately, filling her arms with fruit and flowers. "Captain
Church is certainly good to us," Mollie commented as they
were leaving one day, "and you know, Papa, you look just like
him." It was then that she learned that the Captain was her
grandfather and that her father had been his slave.

While Mollie's parents tried to insulate her from the past,
her grandmother, Eliza Ayres, gave her some perception of her
African heritage. Grandma Liza, a marvelous storyteller, kept
Mollie enthralled with tales of Brother Rabbit and Brother Fox
and a hoop snake who, tail in mouth, rolled after naughty children. But she also told stories about cruel masters and slave
children who were sold away from their parents. Her dramatic
description of an overseer who had once chased her with an

upraised whip always brought Mollie to tears. "Never mind, honey," Eliza would comfort her. "Gramma ain't a slave no more."

Shortly before Mollie's third birthday, the smoldering antagonism between white Memphis and its new black citizens burst into flames. For three days a mob swirled through the streets, murdering, raping, robbing. Fifty black people were killed, over eighty were wounded, and black-owned property valued at more than $100,000 was stolen or destroyed. On the second night, policemen with drawn guns broke into Robert Church's saloon. Shooting him when he tried to resist, they drank up his whiskey, then rifled his cash drawer. Friends brought him home, barely alive, with a bullet wound in his head which would pain him all of his life.

Weeks later, when a committee of congressmen came to Memphis to investigate the riot, they interviewed Church. After he described the break-in and identified the policeman who had shot him, an Illinois congressman, puzzled by this ex-slave who looked and talked like a white, asked, "How much of a colored man are you?" "I don't know," Church replied: "very little."

The range of complexions in her family must also have puzzled Mollie. While her father was fair enough to be taken for white, Mama and Grandma Liza were brown, and her own skin was the color of coffee with cream. However, she was not encouraged to ask questions about such matters; she would have to learn about them from experience.

Mollie Church's first encounter with what she would always refer to as "the Race Problem" came when, at the age of five, she was on a trip with her father. Although there were no laws segregating train passengers at that time, black people were expected to sit up front in the Jim Crow car. Characteristically, Robert Church installed his daughter in the first-class coach before retiring to the smoker for a cigar. Neatly dressed, with blue ribbons bobbing on her braids, Mollie was on her best behavior, remembering her mother's injunction to act "like a little lady." She was startled when the conductor, coming by to collect tickets, told her that she would have to move to the car ahead, "where she belonged."

"Whose little nigger is this?" he asked, as he roughly pulled her from her seat.

Mollie was standing in the aisle, frightened and humiliated, when her father returned and, in a commanding tone, ordered the conductor to leave her alone. The man obeyed reluctantly, but continued to glare at her for the rest of the trip. Why had this happened? Had she done something wrong? And what had the conductor meant by "nigger"?

Her father ignored her questions, forbidding her to discuss the incident. As soon as she returned home, she turned to her mother for enlightenment. Hiding her own dismay, Louisa Church assured Mollie that she had not misbehaved, but that sometimes conductors were unkind and treated good little girls badly. The explanation silenced Mollie, but it did not satisfy her. Years later, when she had daughters of her own, she understood her mother's evasion. "Seeing their children wounded by race prejudice is one of the heaviest crosses which colored women have to bear," she wrote.

Soon after the train encounter, Mollie had to face a different kind of hurt. Her parents were divorced; she and her younger brother, Thomas, went to live with their mother in a house on Court Street, a block away from the hair store. Divorces were uncommon then, and Mollie, wondering if she were somehow responsible, was pained and embarrassed by the separation. The pain was eased by frequent visits from her father, who came by in his buggy to take her to dinner, or turned up at school with a doll he had bought for her—thereby ending all lessons for the day.

School Days

Most of Memphis's schools for black children had been destroyed during the riot. The school that Mollie attended, in the basement of a church, was so inadequate that her mother decided to send her to the North for an education. In the fall of 1870, Mrs. Church took seven-year-old Mollie to Yellow Springs, Ohio, to enroll her in the Model School on the campus of Antioch College. Mollie remained there for five years, boarding with the Hunsters, a black couple who were the proprietors of the town's only hotel and ice cream parlor. Warm and loving people, with grown daughters of their own, the Hunsters became Mollie's surrogate parents. Pa Hunster took her along when he drove to farms in the country to buy cream and eggs, while Ma was always ready to help with snarled hair, back buttons, or knotty homework problems.

Christmas brought wonderful boxes of gifts from her mother. Louisa Church, who had left Memphis to open a hair store in New York, devoted weeks before the holiday to selecting dresses and dolls, jewelry, candy—everything that her small daughter would need and enjoy. In the summertime, before Mollie was old enough to travel alone, she spent her vacations in Yellow Springs. She helped in the ice cream parlor, read all the children's books that the Sunday-school library had to offer, and explored a ravine at the edge of town, where a waterfall brought comfort on hot days. When time dragged, Ma Hunster assigned her poems to memorize, and then listened patiently while she recited them. Eager to please the adults around her, Mollie was a well-behaved child, but never a "goody goody," she said. Bursting with energy, she found it difficult to keep quiet in school and church. Outdoors, she ran, skated, swam, and climbed trees—an activity that had to be pursued in secret, because "nice girls" weren't supposed to show their legs in the 1870s.

The fact that Mollie was the only black child in her grade imposed special burdens. Although she met little overt discrimination, she was occasionally reminded that she was different. Once an older girl made fun of her dark skin. With a rare flash of anger, Mollie retorted that she didn't want a face that "looked like milk" but preferred to be "nice and dark." Another time she was given the part of a stupid black servant in a school play. Realizing that she was being asked to play the fool, she refused the assignment. These stings made her determined to excel, to show her companions that she was their equal in every way. She stood at the head of her class throughout her years in Yellow Springs.

When Mollie was twelve, her parents sent her to Oberlin, Ohio, to attend high school and then Oberlin College. At first she lived with a black family in town; later she boarded in

Ladies Hall, a college dormitory. Despite the ups-and-downs of adolescence, she flourished in her new environment, seizing every opportunity for fun as well as study. She played tennis, then a new sport, rode horseback, and was an official scorer for the all-male baseball games. Although Oberlin authorities frowned on dancing and forbade the girls to dance with boys, Mollie and her classmates spent the after-supper hours practicing the latest two-steps and polkas. After the director of the Oberlin Conservatory found that she had a fine contralto voice, he encouraged Mollie to join the Musical Union. She sang in the annual church presentation of "The Messiah"; and when the young people went on picnics to Lake Erie, she strummed a guitar, a gift from her father.

Oberlin, founded by abolitionists, admitted its first blacks in 1835, far in advance of other colleges. Before the Civil War, both faculty and students were active in the antislavery struggle, and determinedly egalitarian. After Reconstruction, however, the North as well as the South moved toward Jim Crow. Much of the old good will began to evaporate; and black students complained bitterly of discrimination. Mollie felt little of this, however. In Ladies Hall, she roomed alone or with a black roommate, but at mealtimes, when other blacks were usually assigned to separate tables in the dining hall, she was overwhelmed with invitations to sit with whites. Asked to join Aeolian, a prestigious literary society, she represented it in public debates; she became an editor of the *Oberlin Review*, and was a welcome guest at all social functions. "It would be difficult for a colored girl to go through a white school with fewer unpleasant experiences than I had," she later said.

In part, Mollie Church's acceptance was a tribute to her high spirits and intelligence. But it was also because, during the years of living with strangers, she had schooled herself to ignore small difficulties and sidestep large ones, without losing her self-respect. She first expressed this resolutely cheerful philosophy at her high school commencement. Talking on "Troubles and Trials," she set out to prove that most troubles were imaginary; those that could not be reasoned away could be eased by the exercise of tact and diplomacy. To illustrate her point, she told the story of two monks who had been ordered to walk to a distant city wearing shoes that were filled with peas. The first pilgrim was footsore and weary when he reached his destination; the second was all smiles. Asked to explain his good humor, he replied, "I boiled my peas."

"Boiling her peas," Mollie Church sailed through college, overlooking sexism as well as racism. Oberlin men took a four-year Classical Course leading to the degree of Bachelor of Arts. Most women enrolled in the Literary Course, which lasted only two years and earned them a certificate. Mollie's friends urged her to take the "ladies' course," arguing that the study of Latin and Greek was difficult, as well as unnecessary. Besides, it might spoil her chances of getting a husband; men disliked women who knew too much. "Where will you find a colored man who has studied Greek?" one girl asked.

Mollie worried that she would never find a husband, but signed up for the "gentlemen's course" anyway. Often the only girl in a class with forty boys, she held her own without difficulty. Once, when Matthew Arnold, the noted English writer, visited her class, the professor called on her to read a passage in Greek and then translate it. Afterwards, Arnold expressed astonishment at the quality of her performance. He had been informed by the best scientific authority that the tongue of the African was too thick to pronounce Greek correctly.

During her Oberlin years, Mollie divided her vacations between New York and Memphis. She and her brother were visiting their father in Memphis in 1879, when yellow fever spread through the Mississippi Valley for the second year in succession. As the death toll mounted, people thronged to the depot, abandoning homes and shops to crowd onto trains to the North or West. Robert Church hustled his children back to New York, then returned to the stricken city. While most businessmen believed that Memphis was doomed, he used every penny he could scrape together to buy real estate at bargain prices. As the city recovered over the next decade, Robert Church became the South's first black millionaire.

Church's success brought him into the small circle of black leaders who still had influence in national politics. One friend and business associate was Blanche K. Bruce, United States Senator from Mississippi. When Mollie was seventeen, the Bruces invited her to Washington for the inauguration of President James A. Garfield. Wearing gowns purchased by her mother in New York, she twirled, dipped, and glided at the inaugural ball and at the dances and parties that followed. Although she met congressmen, judges, and diplomats in dazzling succession, the high point of the gala week came when she was introduced to Frederick Douglass. Then United States Marshal for the District of Columbia, and the escort of the president-elect when he took the oath of office, the black leader remained her friend for the rest of his life.

Mollie Church was graduated from Oberlin in 1884, one of three black women to receive a B.A. degree from the college that year. She was disappointed that neither of her parents was able to attend the ceremony. Her mother sent her a striking jet-black dress to wear—black was the prescribed color for the women who completed the "gentlemen's course"—and her father surprised her with his purchase of a palatial new home which had carpeted floors and a mirrored ballroom for parties. Now that she had completed her schooling, he expected her to take charge of his household and entertain his guests. When Mollie proposed teaching in a Memphis school instead, Church flatly forbade it.

"Since he was able and willing to support me, he did not understand why I wanted to do any kind of work. In the South for nearly three hundred years 'real ladies' did not work, and my father wanted his daughter to be a 'lady.' But said daughter had been reared among Yankees and had imbibed the Yankee's respect for work," Mollie later explained. Aware that she had had opportunities that were denied to almost all blacks, she had prepared herself for a life of usefulness, dreaming of the day, she said, "when I could promote the welfare of my race."

Unwilling to make an open break with her father, Mollie spent an idle, restless winter in Memphis, growing increasingly unhappy over the "purposeless existence" she was leading. After her father remarried, she felt free to leave. From her mother's apartment in New York, she wrote to a number of

black schools, applying for teaching positions. By the fall of
1885, she was back in Ohio, on the faculty of Wilberforce University, and idleness was no longer a problem.

Founded before the Civil War by the African Methodist
Episcopal Church, Wilberforce was the first American institution of higher learning for blacks. Despite the fact that it was
called a university, many of its students had had little previous
schooling. For a salary of forty dollars a month, Mollie taught
the basics of reading and writing, as well as college-level min-
eralogy and French. She also served as secretary of the faculty,
played the organ for morning and evening services on Sundays,
and rehearsed the choir one night a week.

Although she enjoyed her contacts with her students, some
of whom were older than she, her happiness was marred by her
father's displeasure. After she wrote to tell him that she was
teaching at Wilberforce, he had replied angrily, upbraiding her
for her disobedience. She had continued to write and had sent
Christmas gifts to his family, which now included a half-
brother, Robert, Jr., but he had rebuffed all attempts at a reconciliation. When school closed for the summer, Mollie decided
to make one more attempt to appease him. Heading for Memphis, she sent a telegram en route giving her arrival time. To
her relief, her father was waiting at the station to greet her—
and nothing more was ever said about women who worked.

After another year at Wilberforce, Mollie Church left to
teach Latin in Washington's Colored High School, then the
foremost public school in the country for black youth. Even
before she set foot in the building, matchmakers were busy
pairing her off with the head of her department, Robert H. Terrell, who had graduated with honors from Harvard. He was not
only that rare being, a black man who knew Greek, but he was
tall, handsome, and a fine dancer as well. Mollie was not un-
interested in young men. The summer before, she had been
squired around Memphis by Lieutenant John Alexander, the
second black graduate of West Point, but she had turned down
his marriage proposal. Now, although she was immediately
attracted to her fellow teacher, as he was to her, she side-
stepped any serious commitment. Her father had offered to
send her to Europe to study; marriage must wait.

On the eve of her departure, in the summer of 1888, she had a moment of panic at the thought of leaving home, job, and Robert, to live in a strange land. "My steamer hat, chair and rug have all been secured. The die is now cast and we sail Saturday," she wrote to a friend. "If I would allow it, I could be very gloomy indeed. It is not so easy to go as I had expected, but one must be brave to accomplish anything."

For two years Mollie lived in Europe, learning French, German, and Italian by staying in pensions where no English was spoken and attending local schools. She spent one summer traveling with her mother, who had won $15,000 in a Louisiana state lottery, and another showing the sights to her father and his new family. Every day afforded a wealth of new experiences. Guidebook in hand, she toured art galleries and museums, attended the opera and theater, and tirelessly explored cathedrals and châteaux. In addition to the joy of learning, there was the special exhilaration of being black outside of the United States. For the first time she was able to perceive people as simply people—tall, short, bright, dull—without the need to classify them by race, or to wonder how they would react to her. Warmly received wherever she went, she found Europeans curious about her ancestry, but never antagonistic. The daughter of her landlady in Berlin called her "schön schwarz"— beautifully dark—and a German baron fell in love with her and wrote to her father to ask for her hand in marriage.

Occasionally she toyed with the idea of remaining in Europe, to escape the "Race Problem." But in the fall of 1890, she returned home with a new sense of mission, and no regrets. Never mind that she was coming back to a Jim Crow job in the Jim Crow capital of her country. Few white women, and fewer blacks, had an education that could equal hers. She would find a way to utilize it independently and honorably.

Woman's Work

Teaching Latin and German in Washington, Mollie renewed her friendship with Robert Terrell. When they married a year later in her father's home in Memphis, the *Age*, a black New York newspaper, pronounced the wedding "the most notable event in colored society for years" and devoted a column and a half to a list of their wedding presents. Even the white papers of Memphis, which seldom printed favorable news about black people, reported the event in detail, describing "the elaborate menu and excellent champagne" and the orchestra "which made the air sweet with its beautiful music."

Marriage brought Mary Church Terrell's teaching career to a close—married women were not permitted to teach in most schools in the country—but she quickly found new challenges. The first came when she started housekeeping. In the 1890s, higher education for women was still controversial, and college graduates were the butt of jokes and caricatures. "The comedians on the stage always represented them as wearing bad-looking, unbecoming hats, dresses with the hem ripped half out, and shoes run down at the heel," she wrote. "And as for cooking! Of course college-bred women knew nothing whatever about that. Women who had studied higher mathematics, the sciences and Greek had so violated the laws of nature that it was never possible for them to learn to do well the work which the Creator had ordained they should do."

The uncomfortable truth was that Mollie Terrell, who had lived in other people's homes from the time she was seven, was ignorant of even the rudiments of domestic work. Nevertheless, she resolved to disprove the charges against college women. In her determination to excel, she attended cooking lectures, pored over cookbooks and housekeeping manuals, scrubbed, swept, and polished until her small apartment shone. After teaching herself to sew, she reupholstered the parlor sofa, then painted the walls and varnished the floors of bedroom and kitchen. By the spring of 1892 she was pregnant, and beginning to read up on child psychology, when she received jolting news from Memphis.

The news was that Tom Moss, who had attended her first birthday parties, who had given her a set of silver oyster forks when she married, was dead, the victim of a lynch mob. The murder of her childhood friend shattered Mollie's usual equanimity. Torn between grief and anger, even doubting the existence of a God who could permit such things to happen, she sought out Frederick Douglass. While Ida B. Wells denounced the lynching in the columns of *Free Speech*, Mary Church Terrell and Frederick Douglass visited the White House to ask President Benjamin Harrison to condemn lynching in his annual message to Congress. Although Douglass "eloquently pleaded the case for antilynching legislation," she recalled, the president took no action. Thirty years later, Mary Church Terrell was still working for a law to stop lynching, still remembering Tom Moss.

The lynching, followed by the death of her newborn baby several months later, ended Mary Church Terrell's preoccupation with domesticity. Plunging into community affairs, she became, in short order, the president of Bethel Literary and Historical Society, the nation's foremost black cultural organization; a member of the District of Columbia Board of Education—the first black woman in the country to receive such an appointment; and a cofounder of the Colored Women's League of Washington. In 1896, when the League merged with more than a hundred other women's clubs to form the National Association of Colored Women, she was elected its first president. Poised and tactful, well-grounded in parliamentary procedure, and not above politicking when necessary, she remained in office for five years and was then made honorary president for life.

Choosing the motto "Lifting As We Climb," the National Association was concerned with improving conditions in black communities. At a time when few social services were available, the women started kindergartens and day nurseries, night schools, normal schools, and homes for the aged and infirm. In rural areas they taught the basics of hygiene and nutrition; in cities they set up courses in nurses' training.

Mary Church Terrell was at the center of the action, organizing, adjudicating arguments, publicizing the good work. She carried on an extensive correspondence with club leaders, reporting their successes in newspapers and magazines, and traveled thousands of miles each year to address meetings.

She also served as unofficial ambassador to predominantly white women's organizations. A suffragist since her college days, she had always attended the conventions of the National

American Woman Suffrage Association, which were held bi-
ennially in Washington. On one occasion, when members were
preparing a protest against an injustice, she rose to ask, "as a
colored woman," that the resolution include "the injustices of
various kinds of which colored people are the victims." Susan
B. Anthony immediately invited her to word the resolution
which she wished to have included, and to become a member
of the association. A friendship with Miss Anthony which grew
out of this encounter led to a number of invitations to speak at
suffrage meetings. In 1898, when she addressed the association's convention on "The Progress and Problems of Colored
Women," her speech was "a revelation," according to *The Colored American:*

She spoke for a half hour with power and fascination of manner such
as few women possess and the suffragists on the platform were so
proud of their new discovery that they fell upon her neck upon the
conclusion of her speech and kissed her. She was almost covered with
floral offerings. She made a most magnificent appeal for the assistance
of white women in the work of breaking up the obnoxious systems in
the South that tend to degrade colored women—the Jim Crow car, the
convict lease system and other unsavory institutions. The opportunity
offered Mrs. Terrell by Miss Susan B. Anthony to address the most
progressive and brainiest women of our country was no small compli-
ment. That Mrs. Terrell came up to the full measure of her opportunity, none who were present will gainsay.

Terrell's position on the District Board of Education, which
she held for eleven years, was a demanding one. Responsible
for the black schools in one part of the city, she had the power
to hire and fire the staff and to recommend promotions. More
than eighty thousand black people lived in Washington; some
days it seemed as if every one of them was ringing her doorbell
with a problem which needed solving. While parents came to
complain about teachers, and teachers about principals, Mary
Church Terrell struggled to see that the children, white and
black, received a good education. At a time when music was
considered a "frill," she managed to find a salary for a director
of music for the black schools. Another of the many innova-
tions she introduced was Douglass Day, a day set aside to honor

Frederick Douglass so that black pupils could take pride in their history; the Washington schools were the first in the nation to honor a black person.

When Congress, which held the purse strings for the District, cut the appropriations for the black schools, Terrell headed for Capitol Hill to persuade the lawmakers to change their minds. Some of her encounters with them were disheartening. Once she tried to convince a congressman that a black administrator should be paid four thousand dollars a year, the salary that his white counterpart was receiving. "Four thousand dollars!" the congressman snorted. "Why, no colored man in the world is worth that much."

Although this was a busy period for young Mrs. Terrell, it was not always a happy one. Three times in the first five years of her marriage she gave birth, only to have the baby die within a few days. Adding to the depression that followed each death was the suspicion that the infants might have survived, had they not been born in an inferior Jim Crow hospital. When, against her doctor's advice, Mollie became pregnant for a fourth time, Louisa Church insisted that she come to New York, where she could receive the best medical attention. This time the baby lived. Phyllis—named after Phillis Wheatley, the early American black poet—was healthy, bright, and beloved; and her mother faithfully recorded her progress in letters and diaries, from first tooth to first piano lesson.

Throughout her own childhood, when she was separated from her parents and her brother, Thomas, Mollie had dreamed of a large family. As she approached, then passed, her fortieth birthday, she was concerned because Phyllis was growing up as an only child. When Thomas Church needed to find a home for his daughter, the Terrells offered to adopt her. Four years older than Phyllis, little Mary Church was "a pretty, sweet child," wrote her aunt, on the day she joined their household. "I hope we shall be able to rear her properly so that she shall become a fine specimen of good, pure, intelligent womanhood."

The Terrells brought up Phyllis and Mary as sisters, loving them evenhandedly and giving them every possible advantage. Still a teacher at heart, Mollie Terrell made learning a game rather than a grim experience. At the breakfast table, as the girls spooned strawberries, one by one, onto their cereal, she taught them to count. She organized reading-aloud sessions after school and family evenings at the piano, where Papa, too, played and sang. During Washington's hot summers, Mollie took her daughters on vacation trips—to Opequon, Virginia, where they rode plowhorses and learned about farming; to Harpers Ferry to see and climb the Blue Ridge Mountains; and to Martha's Vineyard for their first swimming and rowing lessons.

Absorbing as it was, however, motherhood never became a full-time occupation. Phyllis was still a toddler when the Slayton Lyceum Bureau—the same agency that had approached Ida B. Wells—offered Mary Church Terrell a contract as a professional lecturer. Lectures then were a form of popular entertainment as well as education; people attended lyceums and summertime Chautauquas to hear explorers, authors, and all kinds of celebrities. Seizing the opportunity to publicize the problems and achievements of black people, Mollie agreed to go on tour for three weeks at a time. Her mother, who had recently moved to Washington, cared for Phyllis and Mary during these absences. Terrell prepared each lecture carefully, sugarcoating her message with anecdotes and catchy titles like "The Bright Side of a Dark Subject" and "Uncle Sam and the Sons of Ham." Handsome, fashionably dressed, speaking in a deep, resonant voice which carried to the far reaches of an auditorium, she made a striking impression on her listeners.

"I enjoy doing this kind of work," she wrote in one exuberant letter to her husband. I really feel that I am putting the colored woman in a favorable light every time I address an audience of white people. Then too it would seem almost reckless to deliberately throw one hundred dollars into the fire when it can be made in three weeks very easily." But there were bad days, too, when schedules were bungled, trains were missed, or managers shortchanged her. "It is anything but a snap, this lecture business," she wrote then. "This is a strenuous life I'm leading. I have to get up and take five or six o'clock trains in the morning, when I reach the place at which I pass the night about eleven or twelve. . . . It is a great sacrifice for me to leave home, I tell you. Only a sense of duty to my race and thrift for myself could induce me to sally forth as a lecturer."

Her sense of duty kept her on the lecture platform for more than thirty years. She spoke at leading forums in New York, Boston, Chicago, and Cleveland, and was a familiar figure on college campuses. Braving the indignities of Jim Crow, she also addressed segregated audiences in the South in order to reach people who had never seen an educated black woman before.

Perhaps her greatest success came in 1904, when she went to Germany to address the International Council of Women. Arriving in Berlin—where everyone was curious to meet "die Negerin," the only dark-skinned delegate—she found the German women critical of the English and Americans who planned to speak in English, a language that few of the Europeans understood. Terrell, feeling that she represented not only the black women of the United States but the whole continent of Africa, listened thoughtfully, then scrapped the speech she had written at home and wrote a new one—in German. Isolating herself in her room, with only forty-eight hours to go before the congress started, she translated, polished, and rehearsed her speech, until it was letter-perfect. She was greeted with tumultuous applause when she gave one speech in flawless German and a second in French; "die Negerin" was declared "the hit of the congress." At its close, editors from half a dozen countries pursued her with requests for articles on the "Race Problem" in the United States.

In spite of her success as a lecturer, Mary Church Terrell's real ambition was to become a writer. Ever since her days at Oberlin, she had contributed columns and news stories to the black press and, occasionally, to white publications. She worked on her articles as conscientiously as she did her speeches, filling scrapbooks with clippings on topics which related to black people, interviewing activists, and checking dates and statistics at the Library of Congress. With her facts in hand, she endeavored to present them in a readable, popular style, being careful, as she said, not to "tear passion to tatters." Her writing was often done under difficulties. No sooner would she be seated at her desk than the doorbell would ring, announcing a visitor bent on school board business. Delivery boys brought packages; repair men came to fix appliances; friends from out of town dropped by to chat. Then it was afternoon and the girls were back from school, demanding attention; or guests were expected for dinner and the silver needed polishing. In entry after entry in her diary, she recorded her frustrations: "I want to write, but everything seems to prevent me from doing so. . . . I am doing nothing but preparing for the Christmas season. I have neither the time nor the thought for anything else. . . . I should like to write but something interferes. I can understand why women with families cannot succeed in literature."

Nevertheless, she persevered. For a time she went to the Library of Congress each morning so that she could work without interruptions. She bought a typewriter and taught herself to type; she hired a part-time secretary to help with her correspondence and a domestic worker who took over most household chores. She wrote short stories, planned a novel that would have the impact of *Uncle Tom's Cabin,* and collected material for a history of black women, from the slave ships to the present day. "Nothing like this has ever been attempted," she wrote. "I hope and pray ardently that I shall carry out this intention."

Along with these long-range projects, she wrote exposés of lynching, chain gangs, the barbarous convict-lease system, and "Being a Colored Woman in the United States." Her chatty style was not the stuff that great literature is made of, but it did not fall below the standards of most magazine writing of the day. Yet her stories and articles were rejected as "propaganda" or "too controversial." After making the rounds of editorial offices in New York, she somberly concluded that

there is a "Conspiracy of silence" on the part of the American press, so far as presenting the Colored American's side of the story is concerned. Anybody who makes him ridiculous or criminal can get a hearing, but his struggles and heartaches are tabooed. There is hardly any use, therefore, for a Colored woman who wants to make an appeal for justice through the medium of the short story to make the effort.

Although she continued to write, contributing articles on black musicians, scientists, and historical figures to a few liberal newspapers and magazines, she gave up her dream of writing fiction.

Throughout these years of success and disappointment, Robert Terrell was always in her corner, cheering her on. While friends warned him against allowing his wife to enter public life, predicting disaster for their marriage when she went on the lecture platform, he encouraged her to accept every opportunity to present her views. "I am glad that your trip to Minneapolis was a triumphal one," he wrote when she was on tour. "I am very glad the people appreciate you at your real worth. You deserve all the plaudits heaped upon your devoted head." During her long absences from home, her letters to "My darling husband" were filled with explicit instructions:

Tell Mother that Floy failed to put in two of my nicest white underskirts. Tell Mother to have her look for them right away. . . . Take good care of my papers under that table by my desk. Don't let Phyllis lay destructive hands on them. . . . Read this article on adenoids. Read that part to Mother showing the necessity of giving children with adenoids plenty of fresh air. . . . I am enclosing my trunk check. *Please* give it to the baggage express co. immediately. It is very important that my trunk be home when I get there. . . .

Teaming up with his mother-in-law to keep the household running smoothly, he carried out Mollie's instructions with good humor and teasingly called her "The General Regulator."

Robert Terrell had no reason to feel threatened by his wife's achievements, for his paralleled hers. Studying law at night while teaching school, he had been admitted to the bar shortly after their marriage. In 1901 when President Theodore Roosevelt asked Booker T. Washington to recommend black men for federal jobs, Robert Terrell's name headed the list. Appointed to a four-year term as judge of the Municipal Court of the District of Columbia, he was reappointed five times, retaining the position, even under a Democratic president, until his death.

Characterizing himself as "a race man in the broadest sense," Judge Terrell—by temperament a middle-of-the-roader

(text continued on page 140)

Far right: Mary Church Terrell before bust of Frederick Douglass, 1953. **1:** Awarded the Diamond Cross of Malta in Philadelphia, 1944. **2:** Receiving honorary Doctor of Letters, June 14, 1948. **3:** Detail of poster announcing a Terrell public address, undated. **4:** Photograph taken prior to marriage to Robert Terrell. **5:** With daughter Phyllis, ca. 1910. **6:** Picketing a D.C. store, 1952, at age 89. **7:** Terrell with Thurgood Marshall, recipients of Seagram's Vanguard Society award, ca. 1952. **8:** Crowds lined up for admission to Supreme Court hearings on *Brown* v. *Board of Education,* December, 1952.

MRS. MARY CHURCH TERRELL
OF WASHINGTON, D. C.

This noble and wonderful woman of the 20th Century will Speak at the

3 **MT. HERODEN BAPTIST CHURCH**

6

GIVE THE GIFT OF DEMOCRACY TO WASHINGTON FOR CHRISTMAS
Don't buy at **KRESGE'S**

Don't buy at **KRESGE'S** The *only* Jim Crow Dime Store on 7th Street

7

MARY CHURCH TERRELL

—was an early supporter of Booker T. Washington, who had become the most powerful black man in the country. The principal of Tuskegee Institute in Alabama, Washington urged blacks to forget about the struggle for equal rights and to concentrate instead on acquiring wealth and respectability. His policy of accommodation with the South made him popular with white businessmen and politicians; throughout the presidential terms of Theodore Roosevelt and William Howard Taft, he had the final say on all black appointments to federal office.

Mary Church Terrell, who was intensely loyal to her husband, found much to admire in Washington and his program. Visiting Tuskegee in 1903, she returned filled with enthusiasm for the school, where students were taught to build houses, to operate sewing machines, and to farm according to modern scientific methods. During the next years, when people like W. E. B. DuBois, an Atlanta University professor, and Ida B. Wells opposed Washington's takeover of the black press and black protest organizations, Mary Church Terrell usually sided with the Bookerites. She became active in the Afro-American Council after Washington gained control of it, and replaced Ida B. Wells as director of its antilynching bureau. When W. E. B. DuBois was considered for an appointment as assistant superintendent of the District of Columbia's schools, she used her position on the school board to secure the job for a supporter of Washington instead.

However, there were limits to her loyalty. In 1906, President Roosevelt summarily dismissed three companies of black soldiers accused of taking part in a shooting incident in Brownsville, Texas. Instead of waiting for a court martial, Roosevelt ordered the men discharged without honor, and barred them from reenlisting. While Booker T. Washington attempted to apologize for the president, most black Americans were shocked by the harsh sentence.

Mary Church Terrell was wondering how best to lodge a protest when her newly-installed telephone rang for the first time. Her caller was the president of the Constitution League, an interracial civil rights group with headquarters in New York. He asked her to go to the War Department to urge Secretary of

War William Howard Taft to suspend the order until an investigation could be made. Springing into action immediately, she waited outside of Secretary Taft's office until he agreed to see her. Her plea on behalf of the soldiers was so effective that Taft cabled Roosevelt, then out of the country, to ask for authority to delay the dismissals. The delay permitted a Constitution League lawyer to go to Brownsville to hear the soldiers' side of the story. Armed with this testimony, Mrs. Terrell and the lawyer went to the White House after Roosevelt's return. Despite their appeal, however, the president refused to reinstate the soldiers.*

The Brownsville incident led Mary Church Terrell to reexamine her attitude toward Booker T. Washington. While she was not ready to join his opponents, whose voices were often too strident for her taste, she began to criticize his acceptance of discrimination. Her persistent campaign on behalf of the Brownsville soldiers and her later critical speeches aroused displeasure at conservative Tuskegee. "Someone ought to muzzle Mary Church Terrell," one Bookerite declared. The displeasure became more pronounced when Mrs. Terrell attended the founding conferences of the National Association for the Advancement of Colored People in 1909 and 1910. The new protest organization, an alliance of white and black liberals, posed a genuine threat to Booker T. Washington's long-standing dominance of black affairs. He wrote to Judge Terrell to point out that Mrs. Terrell's "embarrassing" affiliation with the NAACP, an organization likely to attack President Taft, might make the judge's reappointment to the bench more difficult. "Of course, I am not seeking to control anyone's actions," he concluded, "but I simply want to know where we stand."

Mary Church Terrell had finally decided where she stood. She was convinced that black people needed a national organization which would fight for equal rights. When her husband passed along Washington's warning, she replied that she would

*In 1972, sixty-six years after the incident in Brownsville, the Army announced that the dismissal of the soldiers had been "a gross injustice" and rescinded the dishonorable discharges. Two ex-soldiers, aged 86 and 89, the only known survivors, received American flags and permission to be buried in a national cemetery.

not be deterred "from doing something to help remove the awful conditions which injure you and me and all the rest of us." Although she still disliked some of Washington's critics, she declared that "they shall not stand between me and the principles in which I believe with all my heart and for which I am willing to suffer, if need be, and work."

After serving on the NAACP's executive committee for some time, Mrs. Terrell organized a District of Columbia branch and became its vice-president. The NAACP, in its early years, fought against lynching and racial violence, but could make little headway against the day-by-day discrimination that black people faced. Washington had changed greatly since Mollie Church danced at President Garfield's inaugural ball. Once known as "the colored man's paradise," the capital had become a rigidly segregated city. Blacks who wished to go to the theater or a concert were relegated to a shabby "Colored Gallery"; they were not permitted in downtown hotels or restaurants, and had difficulty buying homes outside of slum areas. Streetcars were segregated; so were all railroads leaving the city for the South.

With no civil rights laws to protect them, blacks had to cope with discrimination as best they could. Because the Jim Crow cars on trains lacked sleeping accommodations, a person planning a long trip usually tried to reserve a berth in a Pullman car. This had to be done surreptitiously—by sending a messenger to the railroad station ahead of time, or asking a light-skinned friend to purchase the tickets. The first time Mary Church Terrell filled lecture engagements in the South, she made up her mind not to get Pullman reservations. "I argued that I was no better than other colored women. If they had to travel without them, I would also," she wrote. But after sitting up all night for three nights in dirty, smoke-filled cars, she decided that she would either have to turn down southern lecture dates or obtain berths in the future.

Even after she began to travel first-class, there were disagreeable experiences. Once, a change in train schedules left her stranded in Texarkana, Texas, after dark. Mistaking her for white, the conductor sent her to a hotel across the street from the station. It had never occurred to her to stop at a hotel for

white people in the South, but before she could come up with
another solution, she found herself at the desk, signing her
name in the register.

"When I registered," she said, "the clerk probably attributed
my swarthy complexion to the smoke and dust which had
blown in through the car window. In my room, I actually hesitated over washing my face for fear that when it was clean, I
should be 'discovered' and ejected from the hotel." Dinner was
another ordeal. Would the people she was seated next to realize
that they were sharing a table with "a monster in the shape of a
real, live, honest-to-goodness colored woman"? But nothing
untoward happened, and she retired to her room for the night.
As she locked the door, she realized with a sudden pang that she
had signed her full name in the register. She had been lecturing
in the South for several weeks and the black newspapers had
carried full reports of her speeches. What would happen if a
hotel employee recognized her name and told the manager?

She finally managed to fall asleep, only to be awakened by
a knock on the door. " 'Your time has come' was the first
thought that popped into my head," she recalled. "I was sure
that the proprietor had learned that I was colored and had come
to wreak vengeance upon me for daring to violate the customs
of the Southland." When she did not answer, a second knock
sounded, louder than the first. Then she remembered that Texarkana had been the scene of a particularly vicious lynching
some years earlier. Resolving not to allow herself to be taken
from the room by a mob, she decided to jump from the balcony
outside her window. "If that did not kill me, it might stun me
enough to prevent me from being sensitive to pain," she
thought. By the time she heard a third knock, she mustered up
the strength to ask "Who is it? What do you want?"

"Lady," a soft voice said, "Did you ring for a pitcher of
water?"

The long night finally came to an end, and she traveled on to
lecture as scheduled, but she never forgot Texarkana. Back in
Washington, there were many times when she passed theaters
and concert halls, pausing to look at the advertisements of
performances that prejudice prevented her from seeing. The

first time that she had to tell Phyllis and Mary that there were places they were forbidden to go was a heartbreaking experience. But as the girls grew older and she wanted them to make the most of the cultural opportunities that the city offered, she developed a bolder attitude toward Jim Crow. When there was a play that she thought worthwhile, she taught them to walk up to the box-office and ask for orchestra seats, counting on their light complexions to mislead the ticket-seller.

"I impressed upon them that they would perpetrate a great injustice if they failed to take advantage of anything which they had a right to enjoy because of arbitrary laws," she said. "The idea of trying to hoodwink even those who imposed unjust restrictions was very distasteful. Inwardly I rebelled against being obliged to play such a role with all the self-respect which a woman who was trying to teach high ideals would naturally have. I hated to teach my children to use such an unpleasant subterfuge. But what was I to do?"

After Phyllis and Mary understood the situation, they were more daring than their mother. Whenever they went to a theater, they made a point of taking a darker-skinned friend with them. One of the Terrells would buy the tickets; then the girls would lock arms and march past the ticket-taker together. They were so self-assured that they were never stopped. Despite their defiance of Jim Crow—which helped them to avoid the feelings of inferiority that the system fostered—Mollie was disturbed because they were growing up in a segregated society. When her father died in 1913, leaving her a share of his estate, she used some of her income to take her daughters to Oberlin for a year. There, with Mary in college and Phyllis at Oberlin Academy, she felt that they had "the same chance of measuring arms with white youth" that she had had.

During World War I, when women were urged to take government jobs to ease a shortage of civilian workers, Mrs. Terrell applied for a clerkship in the War Department. Filling out the standard application form, she wrote "American" when she came to the question that asked "Race." The officer who interviewed her was so impressed with her knowledge of French and German that, failing to look at her closely, he assigned her to work in a white division. Blacks had worked alongside whites in government offices since emancipation, but this, too, was changing, particularly after the election of Woodrow Wilson, the first Democratic president in two decades. Southern-born himself, Wilson had appointed a number of southerners to cabinet posts; they brought their regional prejudices with them.

Mrs. Terrell kept her job for two months, until someone recognized her. Then, charged with inefficiency and creating "considerable disturbance," she was sent to an all-black department. Further humiliation was in store for her when, after a transfer to the Census Bureau, she was notified that she could no longer use the same toilet that the white women used. Protesting to the director of the bureau, she was told that the order was necessary because "colored people associate with thieves and harlots." She handed in her resignation, noting in her diary, "How I loathe these intolerable conditions."

Mary Church Terrell's encounters with segregation in federal departments came at a time when she was closely allied with a number of forward-looking white women. In the last years of the war, as the votes-for-women struggle reached a climax, she and Phyllis joined the team of pickets who, under the auspices of the National Woman's Party, maintained a silent vigil in front of the White House. Month after month the women stood at the gates holding up banners which asked, "Mr. President, What Will You Do for Woman Suffrage?" and "How Long Must Women Wait for Liberty?" At war's end, when women around the world banded together to work for a just and lasting peace, Mrs. Terrell was one of thirty Americans invited to the International Congress of Women which was to meet in Switzerland while the official peace negotiations were under way in Paris.

On the boat to Europe, she sat at the captain's table with such distinguished women as Jane Addams, who was president of the Congress, Florence Kelley, Dr. Alice Hamilton, and Emily Balch. She shared a hotel room in Paris with Jeannette Rankin, the first United States Congresswoman, noting in her diary, "The expense is great, but it is best to do it." At the Congress—where she was once again the only black woman—

her speech was so enthusiastically received that she wrote to
her husband,

If I die tonight, I will not have lived in vain. What did I say? Well, I
told the plain unvarnished ugly truth in as strong German as the
words in that language enabled me to set it forth. I was just. I thanked
the broad-minded white women of the United States for inviting me
to the Congress. I said it was my duty as well as a great pleasure to
admit that many white people help Colored people in every way they
can, and then I went on for fifteen minutes and revealed to those
foreigners the fearful injustices of every description perpetrated upon
Colored people.

Although the white women leaders in the United States
were invariably cordial, going out of their way to prove that
they had no prejudice against Mrs. Terrell, there were times
when she winced at their lack of perception. Even Jane Addams, whom she looked up to as the most progressive woman
in the country, showed herself insensitive on one occasion.
Miss Addams was scheduled to speak to a black group in Washington, and Mrs. Terrell had called to escort her to the meeting.
"Miss A. did not know it was a dinner till I told her. 'Is it all
right for me to eat in a colored hotel in Washington?' she asked,
a bit agitated. I assured her that it was. 'They cross over the
line in Chicago,' she said, 'but I did not know they did it here.'
I assured her they did it here," Mrs. Terrell concluded her diary
entry, without further comment.

Other activist white women proved even more disappoint-
ing—most notably, the suffragists. In the spring of 1919, when
the woman suffrage amendment had passed the House and was
under consideration in the Senate, a federation of black
women's clubs asked to join the National American Woman
Suffrage Association. Fearful that a black affiliation would
antagonize the South and thus jeopardize the final vote in the
Senate, Ida Husted Harper, historian and publicist of the
women's movement, called on Mrs. Terrell to persuade the
clubwomen to withhold their application for a time. "The proposed federal amendment applies to colored women exactly as
it applies to white women," Harper pointed out. "If it fails,
both alike will remain disfranchised."

The clubwomen agreed to delay their application. Some southern senators voted for suffrage—and the Nineteenth Amendment finally passed. However, politicians in the Deep South were quick to announce that they were not going to permit black women to vote. Black men had been barred from the polls by a series of discriminatory laws since the 1890s. After women won the vote, the governor of Georgia declared, "I shall urge the enfranchisement of all white women and the disfranchisement of all black women on the same plan that Negro men are now disfranchised."

When the members of the Woman's Party held a victory celebration in Washington in 1921, Mary Church Terrell decided to collect on past promises. Acting as spokesperson for a group of black women, she called on Alice Paul, leader of the party, whom she had known from her days on the picket line. Terrell read aloud a statement urging that Congress investigate the disfranchisement of black women in the South.

"What do you women want me to do?" Alice Paul asked.

"I want you to tell us whether you endorse the enforcement of the Nineteenth Amendment for all women," Mrs. Terrell replied.

"She refused to say she did. The colored women were disgusted," she later wrote. "Alice Paul displayed the most painful lack of tact I had ever seen."

But Terrell was not yet ready to give up. She brought the statement to the Resolutions Committee of the Woman's Party to ask for its support. "I said colored women need the ballot to protect themselves because their men cannot protect them since the Fourteenth and Fifteenth amendments are null and void. They are lynched and are victims of the Jim Crow laws and other evils."

The response was far from what Terrell had hoped. She was especially shocked at the reactions of two of the women to the story of a lynching in which "a colored woman, two months before she was to become a mother, had her baby torn from her body." One woman asked what the pregnant woman had done to precipitate the lynching; the other commented, "She did something, of course."

At a ceremony at a Washington hotel, Mary Church Terrell and her daughter were given distinguished service medals—pins in the shape of a picket sign—for the part they had played in the passage of the Nineteenth Amendment. But the day when the women's movement was to unite firmly behind the concerns of black and white sisters still lay in the future. The Woman's Party voted to devote itself exclusively to the fight for equality under the law and in the family, and ignored the special disabilities that black women faced.

Carrying On

Through the 1920s, Mary Church Terrell continued to fill her days with people and important causes. She served on the executive committee of the Women's International League for Peace and Freedom, was president of the Southwest Community House, a settlement house in Washington, and was a member of the District's Advisory Council on Playgrounds and Recreation. She went to Capitol Hill to testify before a Senate committee which was considering the antilynching bill, and to protest against overcrowding in the capital's black schools.

After a race riot in Washington, she sprang to the defense of a black woman who had been accused of killing a policeman. Calling on the district attorney who was prosecuting the case, she found that he had grave doubts about the woman's guilt. Although he agreed to tell the jury this, he failed to keep his promise. The woman was convicted of manslaughter—"the most unjust verdict ever rendered!" Terrell wrote in her diary. "I rushed to see Judge Gould and begged him to be merciful. He promised to do so when he sentenced her. I saw Assistant District Attorney Van Dorn and said, 'Here is that wretched man who convicted that poor innocent girl.' He said he only wanted to show both sides of the case!"

The passage of the Nineteenth Amendment propelled her into politics. In 1920, when women voted for the first time, Terrell was appointed director of Work among Colored Women in the East for the Republican National Committee. Working out of the committee's headquarters in New York, she spent her days convincing women that they must use their franchise.

"Hold meetings!" she told her district captains. "Every time
you meet a woman talk to her about going to the polls. However much the white women need suffrage, colored women
need it more." Nights and weekends she traveled from Massachusetts to Delaware to make speeches. Admiring the "snappy
campaign stuff" at one of her rallies, a newspaper reported:
"The meeting was preceded by a street parade. Each woman
was dressed in white and carrying a flag and stepping in proud
time to the music. After the women had taken their seats, the
band played 'The Star-Spangled Banner' and Mrs. Mary Church
Terrell, the speaker of the evening, marched up the aisle while
the audience stood and waved flags."

At campaign time she worked closely with her half-brother,
Robert R. Church, Jr., a Republican national committeeman
from Tennessee and one of the few black Southerners with
some political power. The South was solidly Democratic, but
Republicans like Church had influence at national conventions, where the candidate for president was chosen. Months
before an election, Church came North to work for the party;
afterwards, he stayed on in Washington to see that the blacks
in his region, and on a national level, received a share of federal
jobs. Usually he brought his family with him, and the Churches
and Terrells traveled together to the banquets and balls—most
of them segregated now—which heralded the inauguration of
a new president.

As an increasing number of women entered the political
arena, Mary Church Terrell's organizational talents and her
ability as a public speaker were in demand. In 1929, when Congresswoman Ruth Hanna McCormick decided to run for the
United States Senate—the first time that a woman had entered
a senatorial race—she asked Mrs. Terrell to come to Illinois to
take charge of her campaign among black women. While Chicago black women, including Ida B. Wells, protested mightily
because an "outsider" had been brought in, Mrs. Terrell spent
the months before the election traveling through the state lining up votes for McCormick. Three years later, she was in New
York, to work for the reelection of Herbert Hoover, under the
auspices of the Republican National Committee.

Even after 1936, when large numbers of northern blacks shifted from the party of Lincoln to the party of Franklin D. Roosevelt, Terrell saw no reason to switch her allegiance. Southern Democrats still controlled Congress; and Roosevelt, bowing to political expedience, took no steps to end segregation in Washington or elsewhere. Although she came to admire Eleanor Roosevelt, who was far more liberal than her husband on racial issues, she never supported FDR. In 1940, when FDR ran for a third term, Mary Church Terrell was at the Republican convention in Philadelphia, writing to a friend, "I'm here telling the Republicans whom to nominate for president."

During these years of political involvement, major changes were taking place in the Terrells' household. Both of their daughters married, Mary moving to Chicago and later to California, while Phyllis, who taught music in the District schools, remained in Washington. Then Robert Terrell had a stroke which left him an invalid. Shuttling between hospital and home, he taught himself to walk again with crutches and cane, and to write with his left hand. He continued to be mentally alert and cheerful, keeping up with his judicial work until his death in December 1925.

Outwardly, at least, Mary Church Terrell did not let her husband's death alter the course of her life. Several years earlier, she had bought a fine, big house at 1615 S Street, in a neighborhood that had just opened up to blacks. After Judge Terrell died, she remodeled the house into three apartments, renting out the top floor and reserving the second for Phyllis and her husband. With Mary a frequent visitor, the house was lively with young people. Welcoming their company, Mollie Terrell dispensed equal doses of love and advice. Weekends and summers everyone accompanied her to Highland Beach, a resort in Maryland where she had a summer home overlooking Chesapeake Bay. There she learned to drive a car, weeded the garden wearing a pair of her son-in-law's trousers, and swam daily in the bay. "I can swim better than ever," she gleefully reported.

People who met Mary Church Terrell for the first time might have thought her austere. A dynamic and positive woman with a tendency to domineer, she was also tenderhearted to an extreme. All her life she had gone out of her way to help unfortunate children; she habitually stopped drivers who were maltreating their horses and rescued dogs who had been left in the hot sun without water. An attempt to raise chickens in her backyard failed because she could not bear to eat them. On the day that she sold her hens, she wrote, "While I was catching them and tying their feet I was weeping inwardly. They are my feathered children. I raised them."

By the time she was in her sixties she'd had her share of infirmities, traveling twice to the Mayo Clinic in Minnesota for operations and facing up to the troublesomeness of false teeth and failing sight. But she resisted aging with vigor and determination. She was sixty-eight when she fell in love again. "Something like a miracle has been wrought," she wrote in her diary. "I am enjoying a wonderful friendship. Life without it would be dreary indeed." Since the man in question was married, and prominent in public affairs, there was little hope for a permanent relationship; but for a time she waited for phone calls and letters as eagerly as a young girl, filling her diary with discreetly-worded reports: "Phone call this afternoon: 'I'm glad you haven't forgotten me.' 'That would be impossible.' . . . My company and I enjoyed ourselves as usual and he left about 9. . . . No call today. . . . My friend said last night that he liked the dress and the woman in it. . . . He leaves tomorrow night for the west. . . ."

When her brother died suddenly, and she became guardian of his nine-year-old son, Thomas, Jr., she found a new emotional attachment. No matter that she was seventy-three by then. Without hesitation, she brought the boy to Washington to live with her. Fussing over him, loving him, she shepherded Thomas through school and college.

Neither age nor new responsibilities seemed to give her pause. Her compelling voice was still heard at forums and college commencements in the South and East. In 1937 she traveled to England to address the International Assembly of the World Fellowship of Faiths. In London, she was entertained by Lady Astor, the first woman to serve as a member of Parliament, and she took tea with Emperor Haile Selassie of Ethiopia.

During the depression of the 1930s she worked for six months as a clerk in the Emergency Relief Administration, losing her job after her supervisor discovered that she was not white. When the Daughters of the American Revolution refused to permit the brilliant black contralto Marian Anderson to sing in Constitution Hall, Mary Church Terrell joined with Cabinet members and Supreme Court justices to sponsor the historic concert that Miss Anderson gave on the steps of the Lincoln Memorial.

Mrs. Terrell had contributed articles to *The Journal of Negro History* since its founding in 1916; she wrote newspaper pieces about black soldiers who had fought in the American Revolution, and a pageant based on the life of Phillis Wheatley which was performed in Washington and Baltimore schools. For more than two decades she had worked on a book that she planned to call "The Confessions of a Colored Woman." "If properly done it will be the sensation of the year. The first time a woman has ever done such a thing. Be sure to be courageous and tell everything—Write anonymously—I will do it!!!" she told herself in 1919. Between lectures, committee meetings, and family duties, she wrote, revised—and collected rejection slips. When the book was published at last in 1940 as *A Colored Woman in a White World*, it fell short of her expectations. Although she was critical of American society, she had not been able to bring herself to "tell everything." Throughout her life she had suppressed her anger, schooling herself to meet rebuffs, she said, "with a kind of rebellious resignation and a more or less genuine smile." The smile made white people feel comfortable in her presence, but it kept the book from having the fire and bite that she often revealed in her diaries.

Nevertheless, as the first published full-length autobiography of a black woman, *A Colored Woman in a White World* was respectfully reviewed—too respectfully, its author sometimes thought. Reviewers and feature writers alike treated her as a legendary figure, reporting her achievements in the past tense, as if they were writing an obituary. But Mrs. Terrell was not yet ready for the past tense. "I do not feel old," she insisted, adding wistfully, "I can dance as long and as well as I ever did, although I get very few chances to do so." No one asked her to dance, but as she entered her eighties, each passing year brought new honors. During World War II she was invited to christen a Liberty ship. Poising herself carefully, she broke a bottle of champagne across its prow to name it the S.S. *Harriet Tubman.* After the war, testimonial luncheons were followed by testimonial teas and testimonial banquets. She was feted at the fiftieth jubilee of the National Association of Colored Women, honored by the National Council of Negro Women, and awarded the degree of Doctor of Letters by Oberlin, Wilberforce, and Howard.

Wearing her mortarboard at an audacious angle, Dr. Terrell applied for membership in the American Association of University Women. She was not surprised when a curt letter from the membership chairman of the Washington chapter rejected her application. Believing that "I would be an arrant coward unless I opened the way for other colored women," she appealed to the AAUW's national board. In 1949, after three years of arguing among themselves, the members of the association voted to welcome black women "with open arms."

Times were changing, but never fast enough. Mary Church Terrell could now attend meetings of the American Association of University Women, but she still could not buy a cup of coffee in a restaurant, dime store, or drugstore in the shadow of the Capitol, nor could she attend a theater or concert without deception. Shortly after her AAUW victory, she received a new invitation. She was asked to be honorary chairwoman of the Coordinating Committee for the Enforcement of the District of Columbia's Anti-Discrimination Laws. The committee with the cumbersome name had been organized after members of the newly formed Progressive Party and the National Lawyers Guild discovered what Mrs. Terrell already knew—that the District of Columbia, seventy-five years earlier, had passed laws forbidding the exclusion of black people from restaurants, theaters, and public places. Although the laws had never been repealed, they had been omitted from all printings of the statute books since the turn of the century. The Coordinating Committee, a loose organization of church, social, and labor groups, white as well as black, now planned to call on District authorities to enforce the forgotten laws.

Mrs. Terrell refused to be an honorary anything, but became the working chairperson of the Coordinating Committee. Presiding over meetings, speaking at rallies, and even stuffing envelopes, she was the moving force behind the Committee's work. On January 7, 1950, she led a four-person expedition to Thompson's restaurant, a cafeteria two blocks from the White House. She and her companions managed to put bowls of soup on their trays. Before they could eat, they were asked to leave. That afternoon, Committee lawyers filed a complaint with the Corporation Counsel of the District, charging that Thompson's had violated the old civil rights laws.

While the case made its slow journey through the courts, Mrs. Terrell and Committee members visited the owners of five-and-tens and department stores, hoping to persuade them to open their lunch counters to all comers. After six months of these negotiations, they were able to list twenty-odd restaurants that no longer discriminated. But that left hundreds of others whose owners, following the advice of the powerful Washington Restaurant Association, were determined not to change their policy. Faced with this intransigence, the Committee tried new tactics. They distributed leaflets in front of stores to urge a customer boycott, and then set up picket lines.

The decision to picket was arrived at after some soul-searching. The Korean War had just begun; and the country was entering the McCarthy period, a time of repression when any kind of aggressive action was likely to be labeled "un-American"—a label that could mean loss of a job, blacklisting, and public opprobrium. Some members of the Committee were left-of-center; associating with them might result in charges of disloyalty to the country. But Mary Church Terrell had walked on picket lines and associated with radicals before. On the day that the first pickets gathered in front of a five-and-ten on Seventh Street, she put on her best fur coat and the hat and gloves that the fashions of an earlier day prescribed, and marched at the head of the line. White-haired and stooped, with a cane in one hand and a picket sign in the other, she led the line during December snowstorms and the sweltering days of summer for two years. When she grew tired, she would sit on a folding chair on the sidewalk; but she was always present, directing the action. "When my feet hurt I wasn't going to let a woman fifty years older than I do what I couldn't do," a Committee member said. "I kept on picketing."

One by one, the stores capitulated, and Mrs. Terrell and her fellow pickets were invited to buy pie and coffee at their lunch counters. However, they were still waiting to hear from the Supreme Court. At last, on June 8, 1953, Justice William O. Douglas read the decision: "The Acts of 1872 and 1873 . . . remain today a part of the governing body of laws applicable to the District." "EAT ANYWHERE!" the *Afro-American* proclaimed, in a banner headline. That fall, seven hundred people gathered in the ballroom of a leading hotel to celebrate Mary Church Terrell's ninetieth birthday. After she thanked them in a ringing voice, disdaining the microphone, they pledged to end all race discrimination in Washington by the time she was one hundred.

MRS. TERRELL'S GREAT AGE had freed her from the shackles of public opinion. She was no longer concerned whether something she wanted to do was proper or prudent, but only whether it was right. In the darkest days of the McCarthy period, when people faced jail for membership in radical organizations, her advice to the timid was to "keep on going—keep on insisting— keep on fighting injustice." As a symbol of her new freedom, she broke with the ties of a lifetime to vote for Adlai Stevenson, a Democrat, for president. Defending those who were blacklisted, she continued to ally herself with unpopular causes. When Rosa Lee Ingram, a Georgia sharecropper, and her two sons were sentenced to death for killing a white man who had attacked them, she agreed to head a National Committee to Free the Ingram Family. After leading a delegation to the United Nations, she traveled to Georgia in her ninety-first year to seek a pardon from the governor. The pardon was not granted, but the activities of the committee served to keep the case in the public eye. The Ingrams were finally set free in 1959.

Rosa Lee Ingram was black, but the woman whose name figured most in the news at this time was white Ethel Rosenberg who, along with her husband, had been convicted of giving atomic secrets to the Russians and was scheduled to die in the electric chair. When the committee seeking to save the lives of the Rosenbergs asked for Mrs. Terrell's support, she could easily have rejected their appeal. Instead, she decided to look into the case further. After reading the full record of the Rosenberg trial, she concluded that their conviction was "outrageous." Ignoring the raised eyebrows of her friends, she spoke on the Rosenbergs' behalf at a public meeting in New York.*

Still bright-eyed and alert, she coped with the inroads of old age with resolute good humor. When deafness required her to wear a bulky hearing aid, she made no attempt to conceal it. At a formal dinner party she demonstrated it to a friend, explaining, "It's a great help. I can turn the thing off when I want to." On another occasion, a member of one of her committees rang her doorbell early in the day. Usually she was impeccably dressed, her white hair held at the nape of her neck with a decorative comb. But that morning, taken by surprise, she answered the doorbell in her bathrobe, hair disheveled, and dentures missing. "Here you see beauty unadorned," she cheerfully announced.

Nevertheless, there was little doubt that the machinery of her body was running down. More and more often, she checked herself into a nursing home for a week or two, enjoying the luxury of alcohol rubs and breakfasts in bed, but leaving whenever she had a meeting scheduled or a speech to give. In the winter of 1954, she traveled to New York to receive an award, presided at meetings of the Coordinating Committee, and played bridge each week with the members of her Saturday Club. Writing in her diary, her handwriting as steady as ever, she described a White House reception for the Washington branch of the American Association of University Women, and noted with satisfaction that she had been the first to be taken to meet Mamie Eisenhower, the President's wife, while other

*Ethel and Julius Rosenberg were executed on June 19, 1953.

branch members stood in line to wait for the ceremonial hand-shake. The months were clouded by concern for Thomas Church who, after finishing law school, was entering the Army. "I am worrying about Thomas," she wrote again and again. "He leaves me tomorrow. He and I had dinner at Bur-ton's. Perhaps we shall never have another dinner together. . . . Perhaps I shall never see him again."

That summer when she went to Highland Beach as usual, she no longer took her daily swim in the bay. Sitting on the porch with Phyllis and Mary, she planned a fall trip to Georgia to plead again for Rosa Ingram's freedom. The trip was never made, for on July 24, 1954, Mary Church Terrell died. Days later, her body lay in state in the new headquarters building of the National Association of Colored Women. Thousands filed by to pay their last respects and messages of condolence came from all over the world—but Pfc. Thomas Church, stationed in Japan, was unable to come home for the funeral.

About the Author

DOROTHY STERLING, who has written over thirty books since 1951, pioneered in black history for young people with such early titles as *Freedom Train, The Story of Harriet Tubman* and *The Making of an Afro-American: Martin R. Delany, 1812–1885,* and the more recent *Tear Down the Walls! A History of the American Civil Rights Movement* and *Speak Out in Thunder Tones, Letters and Other Writings by Black Northerners, 1787–1865.* One of her best-known books, *Mary Jane,* now translated into six languages, is a fictional account which grew out of interviews Sterling conducted in 1955 with the first black children to attend desegregated schools in the South. She has been the recipient of several literary prizes, including the Carter G. Woodson award of the National Council of the Social Studies, in 1977, for *The Trouble They Seen: Black People Tell the Story of Reconstruction.* Sterling is the editor of *We Are Your Sisters: Black Women in the Nineteenth Century* and *Turning the World Upside Down: The Anti-Slavery Convention of American Women Held in New York City, May 9–12, 1837* (The Feminist Press, 1987). She is currently working on a biography of the abolitionist-feminist Abby Kelley.

About Margaret Walker

Margaret Walker is the author of *Jubilee,* a historical novel based on the experiences of her ancestors, published in 1965. Her poems, which began to win acclaim with the Yale University Younger Poets award, have been collected in three volumes: *For My People* (1942), *Prophets for a New Day* (1970), and *October Journey* (1973). Her *Collected Poems* is being prepared for publication. She is also the author of *The Daemonic Genius of Richard Wright* (1987). A teacher for many years, Walker is Professor Emeritus of English, Jackson State University, Mississippi.

About Barbara Christian

Barbara T. Christian is a professor in Afro-American studies at the University of California, Berkeley. She has written on Afro-American literature, especially on the writings of black women. She is the author of *Black Women Novelists, The Development of a Tradition* (1980) and *Black Feminist Criticism: Perspectives on Contemporary Black Women Writers* (1985). Christian has also developed curriculum in Afro-American and women's studies for the junior high and senior high school classroom and is one of the authors of the multi-ethnic curriculum on women's history, *In Search of Ourselves*, funded under the Women's Educational Equity Act.

Bibliography: Introduction

Bibliographies

Cole, Johnnetta B. "Black Women in America: An Annotated Bibliography." *Black Scholar* 3 (December 1971):42–53.
Davis, Lenwood G. *The Black Woman in American Society: A Selected Annotated Bibliography*. Boston: G.K. Hall, 1975.
Williams, Ora. *American Black Women in the Arts and Social Sciences: A Bibliographic Survey*. Metuchen, N.J.: The Scarecrow Press, Inc., 1978.

History

Ballard, Allen. *The Education of Black Folk: The Afro-American Struggle for Knowledge in White America*. New York: Harper and Row, 1974. Philosophy of black education from Reconstruction through the early twentieth century.
Blassingame, John W. *The Slave Community: Plantation Life in the Ante-Bellum South*. New York: Oxford University Press, 1972. Study of plantation life focusing particularly on slave personalities. A critique of the Sambo stereotype.
Carson, Josephine. *Silent Voices: The Southern Negro Woman*. New York: Delacorte, 1969. Interviews with black Southern women of different ages and socioeconomic backgrounds.
Cole, Johnnetta. "Militant Black Women in Early U.S. History." *The Black Scholar* 9 (April 1978): pp. 38–45. Discussion of struggles of black women in resisting slavery.
Davis, Angela. "Reflections on the Black Woman's Role in the Community of Slaves." *Black Scholar* 3 (December 1971): pp. 2–15. Essay on the work of slave women and their participation in resisting slavery through overt and covert means.
——. *Women, Race, and Class*. New York: Random House, 1981. Essays that examine the relationship between gender, race, and class, from the perspective of black women's history.
Flexner, Eleanor. *Century of Struggle: The Women's Rights Movement in the United States*. New York: Atheneum, 1971. A by-now classic overview of the women's movement from the colonial period to 1919. Includes chapters on women's education and women and the labor movement. Excellent material on contributions of black women. Little on racism within the suffrage movement.
Franklin, John Hope. *From Slavery to Freedom: A History of Negro Americans*. 3rd ed. New York: Vintage Books, 1969. Comprehensive and useful overview of the history of black Americans.
Genovese, Eugene D. *Roll, Jordan, Roll: The World the Slaves Made*. New York: Vintage Books, 1974. Class analysis of slave system in the United States stressing paternalism as basic characteristic of master/slave relationship.
Giddings, Paula. *When and Where I Enter: The Impact of Black Women on Race and Sex in America*. New York: William Morrow & Co., Inc. 1984.

A history of black women in America from the point of view of their impact on struggles for political, racial, and sexual equality.

Gutman, Herbert G. *The Black Family in Slavery and Freedom, 1750-1925.* New York: Pantheon Books, 1976. Shows cohesion of black family under slavery and the family's importance both during slavery and afterward in maintaining an Afro-American cultural tradition. Refutes many negative myths concerning the black family.

Hams, Middleton Harris, ed. *The Black Book.* New York: Random House, 1973. Pictures and photographs of black Americans. Good sections on lynching and on slave resistance, with some excellent examples of slave women who resisted slavery.

Harley, Sharon, and Terborg-Penn, Roslyn, eds. *The Afro-American Woman: Struggles and Images.* Port Washington, N.Y.: National University Publications, 1978. Excellent collection of essays on history of Afro-American women. Includes essays on the black women's club movement and on racial discrimination within the women's suffrage movement.

Henri, Florette. *Black Migration: Movement North, 1900-1920.* Garden City, N.Y.: Anchor Press/Doubleday, 1975. Important monograph discussing reasons blacks left the South and the discrimination and poor living conditions they found in the North. Also traces the development of black political consciousness during this period.

Horton, James Oliver. "Freedom's Yoke: Gender Conventions among Antebellum Free Blacks." *Feminist Studies* 12, no. 1 (Spring 1986): 51-76. Analyzes relationships between free black woman and men before the Civil War in the domestic and political spheres.

Jordan, Winthrop D. *White over Black: American Attitudes toward the Negro, 1550-1812.* Baltimore: Penguin Books, Inc., 1969. Traces historical roots of racist ideology in America.

Lerner, Gerda, ed. *Black Women in White America: A Documentary History.* New York: Vintage Books, 1973. Writings by and about black women. A basic reference for teachers and students with many excerpts useful for the high school classroom.

———. *The Majority Finds Its Past: Placing Women in History.* New York: Oxford University Press, 1979. Ground-breaking historiographical essays on women's history. Includes essays on black women in the United States, on the relations between black and white women, and on the black women's club movement.

Loewenberg, Bert B.J., and Bogin, Ruth, eds. *Black Women in Nineteenth Century American Life: Their Words, Their Thoughts, Their Feelings.* University Park: Penn State University Press, 1976. Collection of works by black women—slaves, abolitionists, and activists. Excellent bibliography on black Americans.

Meltzer, Milton, ed. *In Their Own Words: A History of the American Negro.* 3 volumes. New York: Crowell, 1964. Documents on Afro-American history.

Quarles, Benjamin. *The Black Abolitionists.* New York: Oxford University Press, 1969. Useful study of black male abolitionists. Relatively little information on women.

Scott, Anne Firor. *The Southern Lady: From Pedestal to Politics.* Chicago: Chicago University Press, 1970. Discusses the contrast between the ideal of the white Southern lady and the reality of life for most southern women.

Sterling, Dorothy. *We Are Your Sisters: Black Women in the Nineteenth Century.* New York: W.W. Norton & Co., 1984. A documentary history of black women in the nineteenth century through their own statements with notes that contextualize their words.

White, Deborah. *A'n't I a Woman: Female Slaves in the Plantation South.* New York: W.W. Norton & Co., 1985. An imaginative historical analysis of the female slave in the South.

Yetman, Norman. *Life under the "Peculiar Institution."* New York: Holt, Rinehart and Winston, 1970. Slave narratives and excellent photographs of slaves.

Biography and Autobiography

Bearden, Jim, and Butler, Linda. *The Life and Times of Mary Shadd Cary.* Toronto: NC Press, Ltd., 1977.

Billingsley, Ray A., ed. *The Journal of Charlotte L. Forten: A Free Negro in the Slave Era.* New York: Dryden Press, 1953.

Brent, Linda. *Incidents in the Life of a Slave Girl.* New York: Harcourt Brace Jovanovich, 1973. Narrative of a woman who escaped slavery.

Cantarow, Ellen, with Susan G. O'Malley and Sharon Hartman Strom. *Moving the Mountain: Women Working for Social Change.* Old Westbury, N.Y./ New York: The Feminist Press/McGraw-Hill, 1980. Three oral histories of women activists, including that of Ella Baker, civil rights activist and one of the founders of the Student Nonviolent Coordinating Committee (SNCC).

Chisholm, Shirley. *Unbought and Unbossed.* Boston: Houghton-Mifflin, 1962.

Conrad, Earl. *Harriet Tubman.* New York: Paul S. Eriksson, 1970.

Duster, Alfreda, ed. *Crusade for Justice: The Autobiography of Ida B. Wells.* Chicago: University of Chicago Press, 1970.

Gaines, Ernest. *The Autobiography of Miss Jane Pittman.* New York: Bantam Books, 1971. Novel told from the point of view of a black woman, covers period from slavery to twentieth century.

Graham, Shirley. *The Story of Phillis Wheatley: Poetess of the American Revolution.* New York: Pocket Books, 1969. Young adult biography of slave who became a famous poet.

Holt, Rackman. *Mary McLeod Bethune.* New York: Doubleday, 1964.

Lorde, Audre. *Zami: A New Spelling of My Name.* Waterton, Mass: Persephone Press, 1982. A poetic autobiography of a contemporary black lesbian feminist writer.

Murray, Pauli. *Proud Shoes: The Story of an American Family.* New York: Harper and Row, 1978. A family history by Pauli Murray—feminist, civil rights activist, lawyer, poet, and most recently, Episcopalian priest.

Pauli, Hertha. *Her Name was Sojourner Truth.* New York: Appleton-Century-Crofts, Inc., 1962.

Petry, Ann. *Harriet Tubman: Conductor on the Underground Railroad.* New York: Pocket Books, 1971.

Porter, Dorothy. "Sarah Parker Remond: Abolitionist and Physician." *Journal of Negro History* 20 (July 1935):287–93.

Terrell, Mary Church. *A Colored Woman in a White World.* Washington, D.C.: Randsell Publishing Co., 1940.

Truth, Sojourner. *Sojourner Truth: Narrative and Book of Life.* Chicago: Johnson Publishing Co., 1970. Biographies, essays, and brief commentary on Sojourner Truth.

Walker, Margaret. *Jubilee.* Boston: Houghton-Mifflin and Co., 1967. A historical novel about a black woman during slavery and Reconstruction by an important black writer.

Wilson, Harriet E. *Our Nig; or Sketches from the Life of a Free Black.* New York: Random House, originally published in 1859, reprinted in 1983 with introduction by Henry Louis Gates. An autobiographical novel by a free black woman of the nineteenth century. Now considered the first novel by a black woman to be published in the United States.

Black Feminism

Cade, Toni, ed. *The Black Woman: An Anthology.* New York: New American Library, 1974. Anthology of contemporary black women's writing on sexism, sex roles, work, motherhood, and women's liberation.

Christian, Barbara. *Black Women Novelists: The Development of a Tradition, 1892–1976.* Westport, Conn.: Greenwood Press, 1980. Literary history of black women's novels from nineteenth century to the present.

────. *Black Feminist Criticism: Perspectives on Black Women Writers.* New York: Pergamon Press, 1985. Collection of essays on black women writing from a developing black feminist perspective.

Davis, Angela. "Rape, Racism, and the Capitalist Setting." *The Black Scholar* 9 (April 1978):24–30. A Marxist critique of recent feminist analyses of rape. Suggests that this writing is often characterized by a traditional racist bias regarding black men and rape.

Ferguson, Renee. "Women's Liberation Has a Different Meaning for Blacks." In Lerner, *Black Women in White America*, pp. 587–91. An important early statement of black feminism.

Foster, Frances. "Adding Color and Contour to Early American Self-Portraitures: Autobiographical Writings of Afro-Americans." In *Conjuring: Black Women, Fiction, and Literary Tradition,* ed. Marjorie Pryse and Hortense Spillers. Bloomington: Indiana University Press, 1985. An essay that discusses the autobiographical writings of nineteenth-century free black women.

Gwin, Minrose. "Green-Eyed Monsters of the Slavocracy: Jealous Mistresses in Two Slave Narratives." In Pryse and Spillers, *Conjuring.* Looks at the relationship between female slaves and slave mistresses in the female slave narratives.

Hood, Elizabeth. "Black Women, White Women, Different Paths to Liberation." *The Black Scholar* 9 (April 1978):45–56. Discussion of differences in historical experiences of black and white women and the effect of these differences on the development of black feminism.

Hooks, Bell. *Ain't I a Woman: Black Women and Feminism.* Boston: South End Press, 1981. A speculative analysis of the relationship between black women and feminism.

——— . *Feminist Theory, from Margin to Center.* Boston: South End Press, 1984. Analysis of black feminist theory.

Hull, Gloria T.; Scott, Patricia Bell; and Smith, Barbara, eds. *All the Women Are White, All the Blacks Are Men, But Some of Us Are Brave: Black Women's Studies.* Old Westbury, N.Y.: The Feminist Press. Groundbreaking anthology of bibliographies, essays, and creative writing on the concept of black women's studies.

Jordan, June. "A Declaration of Independence I'd Just as Soon Not Have." *Civil Wars.* Boston: Beacon Press, 1981. A ground-breaking essay that looks at the ways black women have been left out of the black, women's, and Third World liberation movements.

Lewis, Diane. "A Response to Inequality: Black Women, Racism, and Sexism." *Signs* 3 (Winter 1977):339–61. Analysis of economic and educational opportunities available to black women since the Civil Rights movement and of the socioeconomic reasons for the emergence of a black feminist movement.

Lorde, Audre. *Sister Outsider.* Trumansburg, N.Y.: The Crossing Press, 1984. Collected essays by a black lesbian feminist on issues ranging from the erotic to the uses of anger.

McDowell, Deborah. "New Directions for Black Feminist Criticism." In *The New Feminist Criticism,* ed. Elaine Showalter. New York: Pantheon Books, 1985. Explores issues that comprise a black feminist approach to literature.

Murray, Pauli. "Jim Crow and Jane Crow." In Lerner, *Black Women in White America,* pp. 592–98. An important early statement of the socioeconomic situation of black women and of the existence of sexism within the Civil Rights movement.

Smith, Barbara. "Towards a Black Feminist Criticism." *Conditions Two* (1970). Ground-breaking essay on the need for a black feminist theory.

Walker, Alice. "In Our Mother's Gardens." *Southern Exposure* 4 no. 4:60–65. Beautifully written essay by black novelist, poet, and feminist. Explores how poor black women who were denied education expressed their artistic creativity. Also appeared in *Ms.* 2, no. 11 (May 1974):64–70.

Wallace, Michele. *Black Macho and the Myth of the Superwoman.* New York: The Dial Press, 1979. Controversial book about the need for black feminism through analyzing black women's and men's roles in the Civil Rights and Black Power movement.

Films, Video Cassettes, Records

Alice Walker. The BBC. An excellent study of the writer through a compelling history of her black Southern family.

Autobiography of Miss Jane Pittman. Extension Media Center. 1974. Powerful film in which a black woman recalls her life experiences, spanning the time from slavery to the Civil Rights movement. Stars Cicely Tyson. 120 min.

Fannie Lou Hamer: Portrait in Black. Sterling Educational Films. 1972. An interview with Fannie Lou Hamer, the Civil Rights activist who founded the Mississippi Freedom Democratic Party and organized voter registration campaigns in the South during the sixties. 10 min.

Fundi: The Story of Ella Baker. A documentary on the life of the Civil Rights activist.

Harriet Tubman and the Underground Railroad. Extension Media Center. 1964. Suspenseful film dramatizing Harriet Tubman's adventures as the conductor of the Underground Railroad. Stars Ruby Dee, Ethel Waters, and Ossie Davis. 54 min.

I Am Somebody. Extension Media Center. 1970. Powerful documentary about a successful strike of black women hospital workers in Charleston, South Carolina. 18 min.

Margaret Sloan on Black Sisterhood. Video Cassette. 1974. Public Television Library, 1974. Founder of the National Black Feminist Organization and former *Ms.* editor discusses racism and feminism. 29 min.

The Negro Woman. Folkways Records. FH5523. Speeches of well-known black women including Sojourner Truth, Ida B. Wells, and Frances Ellen Watkins Harper.

To Be Young, Gifted and Black. Extension Media Center. 1972. Adapted from the stage production, this film depicts Lorraine Hansberry's personal and artistic struggles to achieve success as a black female playwright. Based on her plays, letters, and diaries. Stars Ruby Dee, Al Freeman, Jr., and Claudia McNeil. 90 min.

Distributors

Extension Media Center. 2223 Shattuck Ave., Berkeley, CA 94720.
Public Television Library. 475 L'enfant Plaza S.W., Washington, D.C. 20024.
Sterling Educational Films. 241 East 34 St., New York, NY 10016.

Bibliography: Ellen Craft, Ida B. Wells, Mary Church Terrell

Ellen Craft:
The Valiant Journey

Books, Articles:
Bowditch, Vincent Y. *Life and Correspondence of Henry Ingersoll Bowditch.* Boston, 1902.
Brown, William Wells. *The American Fugitive in Europe.* 1855. Reprint. New York, 1969.
Butler, John G. *Historical Record of Macon and Central Georgia.* Macon, 1897.
Child, Lydia Maria. *The Freedmen's Book.* Boston, 1865.
Craft, William. *Running a Thousand Miles for Freedom.* London, 1860.
Farrison, William E. *William Wells Brown,* Chicago, 1969.
Freedman, Florence B. *Two Tickets to Freedom.* New York, 1971.
Frothingham, Octavius B. *Theodore Parker.* Boston, 1874.
Grimke, Archibald. "Anti-Slavery Boston." *New England Magazine,* December 1890.
Martineau, Harriet. *Autobiography.* Edited by Maria Weston Chapman. Boston, 1877.
Mayne, Ethel C. *Life and Letters of Anne Isabella Lady Noel Byron.* New York, 1929.
Siebert, William. *The Underground Railroad from Slavery to Freedom.* New York, 1898.
Still, William. *The Underground Railroad.* Philadelphia, 1871.
Tiffany, Nina Moore. "Stories of the Fugitive Slaves." *New England Magazine,* January 1890.
Weiss, John. *Life and Correspondence of Theodore Parker.* Boston, 1863.
Woodson, Carter G. *The Mind of the Negro as Reflected in Letters Written during the Crisis.* Washington, D.C., 1926.

Newspapers:
The Anti-Slavery Advocate (London): July 1, September 1, 1859.
The Anti-Slavery Reporter (London): September 1, 1860; July 1, September 1, October 1, November 2, 1863; January 1, 1864.
Boston Daily Advertiser: August 22, 1873; July 30, 1875, September 26–28, 1876; June 6–July 16, 1878.
Boston Journal: June 6–July 16, 1878.
The Commonwealth: September 18, October 2, October 23, November 6, November 13, December 25, 1869; August 16, 1873; June 22, 1878.
The Freed-Man (London): December 1, 1865; June 1, July 1, November 1, 1866; March 1, April 1, May 1, 1867.
Georgia Telegraph: February 13, December 28, 1849; November 5, 12, 22, 1850.
Georgia Journal and Messenger: November 6, 13, 26, 1850.

The Liberator: January 12–June 8, 1849; September 27–December 6, 1850; January 24, March 7, May 30, July 18, September 12, September 26, 1851; February 23, 1855; August 4, 1865.

National Anti-Slavery Standard: February 8, 1849; September 11–December 18, 1869; February 5–April 16, 1870.

New National Era: December 14, 1871; January 16, 1873.

New York Globe: April 7, 1883.

New York Times: December 8, 1874.

Woman's Journal: September 27, 1873.

Documents, Letters:

Akers, Samuel L. (former Dean of Wesleyan College). Letters to author.

Boston. Boston Public Library. Anti-Slavery Collection (letters from Ellen Craft, William Craft, Mary Ann Estlin, John B. Estlin, Samuel May, and others).

Boston, Houghton Library, Harvard University. Letter from S. T. Pickard, William H. Siebert papers.

Bryan County, Georgia. 1880 Census Schedule.

De Costa, Julia Craft. Letters to author.

Foley, The Reverend Albert S. (author, *Bishop Healy: Beloved Outcast,* New York, 1954). Letters to author.

Georgia Department of Archives and History. Deed to Woodville.

Ithaca. Cornell University Library. Letters from Lydia Maria Child.

Washington, D.C. National Archives. Letters from William Craft.

Winnett, The Reverend Cannon A. R. (Ockham, England). Letters to author.

Ida B. Wells:
Voice of a People

Books, Pamphlets, Articles:

Aptheker, Herbert. *A Documentary History of the Negro People.* New York, 1951.

Bontemps, Arna, and Conroy, Jack. *Anyplace but Here.* New York, 1966.

Flexner, Eleanor. *Century of Struggle.* Cambridge, 1959.

Fox, Stephen R. *The Guardian of Boston: William Monroe Trotter.* New York, 1970.

Gosnell, Harold F. *Negro Politicians.* Chicago, 1935.

Kellogg, Charles Flint. *NAACP,* vol. 1. Baltimore, 1967.

Meier, August. *Negro Thought in America 1880–1915.* Ann Arbor, 1963.

Papachristou, Judith. *Women Together, A History in Documents of the Women's Movement in the United States.* New York, 1976.

Penn, Garland I. *The Afro-American Press and Its Editors.* Springfield, 1891.

Spear, Allan H. *Black Chicago.* Chicago, 1967.

Thornbrough, Emma Lou. *T. Thomas Fortune.* Chicago, 1972.

Tucker, David M. "Miss Ida B. Wells and Memphis Lynching." *Phylon,* Summer 1971.

Wells, Ida B. Articles by and about in *New York Age, Detroit Plaindealer, Topeka Weekly Call, Indianapolis Freeman,* 1885–1895; *Memphis Appeal Avalanche,* December 25, 1884.

_____. *Crusade for Justice: The Autobiography of Ida B. Wells.* Edited by Alfreda M. Duster. Chicago, 1970.

_____. *On Lynchings.* New York, 1969.

_____. *The Reason Why the Colored American Is Not in the World's Columbian Exposition.* With Frederick Douglass, I. Garland Penn, and Ferdinand L. Barnett, Chicago, 1893.

Manuscripts, Interviews:

Chautauqua. Chautauqua County Historical Society. Albion Tourgee papers.

Chicago. Regenstein Library, University of Chicago. Ida B. Wells papers.

Duster, Alfreda M. Interviews with and letters to author.

Washington, D.C. Library of Congress. Frederick Douglass papers.

Mary Church Terrell:
Ninety Years for Freedom

Books, Articles:

Church, Annette E., and Church, Roberta. *The Robert Churches of Memphis.* Ann Arbor, 1974.

Flexner, Eleanor. *Century of Struggle.* Cambridge, 1959.

Kellogg, Charles Flint, *NAACP,* vol. 1. Baltimore, 1967.

Meier, August, *Negro Thought in America 1880–1915.* Ann Arbor, 1963.

Papachristou, Judith. *Women Together, A History in Documents of the Women's Movement in the United States.* New York, 1976.

Shepperd, Gladys Byram. *Mary Church Terrell—Respectable Person.* Baltimore, 1959.

Render, Sylvia L. "Afro-American Women." *The Quarterly Journal of the Library of Congress,* October, 1975.

Sterling, Dorothy. *Lift Every Voice.* New York, 1965.

Terrell, Mary Church. Articles by and about in Terrell Papers, Library of Congress.

_____. *A Colored Woman in a White World.* Washington, 1940; reprinted 1968.

Woodward, C. Vann. *The Strange Career of Jim Crow.* New York, 1957.

Manuscripts, Interviews:

Langston, Phyllis Terrell. Interviews with author.

Porter, Dorothy. Interviews with author.

Stein, Annie. Interviews with author.

Washington, D.C. Library of Congress. Letters and diaries. Mary Church Terrell papers.

Washington, D.C. Library of Congress. Robert H. Terrell papers.

Index

The numbers in italics indicate pages with illustrations.